1992 AMERICAN GUIDE TO U.S. GOLD COINS

Charles F. French
Edited by John Adler

A FIRESIDE BOOK
Published by Simon & Schuster
NEW YORK LONDON SYDNEY TORONTO TOKYO SINGAPORE

Fireside
Simon & Schuster Building
Rockefeller Center
1230 Avenue of the Americas
New York, New York 10020

Manufactured in the United States of America

10 9 8 7 6 5 4 3 2 1   Pbk.

ISBN 0-671-74806-8 Pbk.

ISSN: 1046-588X

Portions of this work were published in *The American Guide to U.S. Coins.*

CONTENTS

Part One:

SOME HISTORY AND ADVICE

INTRODUCTION

Since the dawn of civilization, gold has been hunted by man! Treasured for its beauty, durability, ease of transportation, and scarcity, it has inspired man to go to heroic lengths to secure it. Its demand made it the first basic commodity in trade. Ancient Egyptians cherished it; King Croesus first struck coins from it; Greeks and Romans buried their hoards of it in earthen jars. The Incas in South America erected statues and made idols out of it. Man throughout all parts of the world sought it.

In ancient times, armies sacked cities for gold and other treasures. During the Middle Ages, walled castles were built to protect such valuables. Vikings sacked England; pirates roved the seas, outlaws robbed; Spain conquered and plundered Central and South America. All for gold and treasures.

The discovery of gold in 1849 in California hastened the settlement of the Far West, caused murders and stagecoach robberies. All in the name of the magic word Gold.

To this day gold continues to be a valuable commodity. Governments use it to obtain foreign exchange, speculators view it as an investment, and numismatists treasure it for its aesthetic value and the history that's expressed in gold coins.

1.

THE FIRST
GOLD COINS
OF THE UNITED STATES

HALF EAGLES

The half eagle, or five-dollar gold piece, was the first gold coin struck by the U.S. Mint in accordance with the Coining Act of April, 1792. Dated 1795, it shows Liberty's head, in a turban-like headdress, facing right. The reverse displays an eagle with spread wings, holding a wreath of laurel in its beak and standing on a palm branch. It is thought that this design was taken from a Roman onyx cameo of the first century B.C. Half eagles were the U.S. Mint's major output. Even so, they were issued in very limited quantities.

QUARTER EAGLES

In addition to half eagles, limited quantities of quarter eagles and eagles were coined, but only on demand.

GOLD DOLLARS AND GOLDEN EAGLES

The reevaluation of U.S. gold coins in 1834 is felt to be responsible for the extreme rarity of our early pieces. It is thought that many were sold back to the mint at the metal's new value, to be melted for recoinage. By weight, each $100 worth of old-type coins would bring at least $106.

The design of the reverse was changed in 1797 to a spread eagle. It was not until 1807, with the second design change, that denominations were placed upon our gold.

The eagle ($10.00) was to be 247½ grains pure, 270 grains standard; the half eagle ($5.00) was to be 123¼ pure, 135 grains standard; and the quarter eagle ($2.50) was to be 61⅞ pure and 67½ grains standard. The standard weight included an alloy to make the coins wear better.

11

These gold coins were pegged to silver on a 15:1 ratio—fifteen ounces of silver to one ounce of gold. But while this ratio was valid at the time the bill was passed, by 1799 the ratio in Europe had reached 15¾:1, and the undervalued coins began to flow out of the country or were melted down for the higher value of their metal. As a result, gold disappeared from circulation, as did silver dollars.

It wasn't until June 28, 1834, that a new law reduced the weight of gold coins. From that time on, our gold pieces appeared in the new smaller size, returned to circulation, and created a new interest in and demand for gold. Gold mines profitably increased their production. Our mint first struck twenty-dollar double eagles and experimented with fifty-dollar coins in 1849. At this time, we also find our first gold dollars appearing, closely followed by threes. The three-dollar gold piece, first coined in 1854, was never a popular coin. It was often associated by the superstitious with bad luck.

The quantities of gold and shortages of gold coins in the West prompted the coinage of pioneer pieces in many denominations. Privately issued and not under rigid regulation, many of these were not up to standard fineness; as late as the latter part of the 1920s, these pioneer pieces were looked down upon as low-grade, overvalued coins and were redeemed by financial institutions at less than face value. Today, these low-grade coins are rare and worth high premiums, not for their gold value but for their numismatic value.

From the time shortly after the Civil War until the banking holiday in 1933, numismatic interest in collecting gold coins was not high. Anyone who wanted to collect them could easily have secured coins of most denominations for very little above face value, even those from as far back as 1834, when the new smaller size was adopted. A great many of the first gold pieces prior to 1804 could be purchased for much less than their rarity should have dictated.

Proof gold coins (see Chapter 6) were not popular with collectors. Until the last few years, only twenty-five to forty proof gold dollars were struck in most years. Similar small quantities were coined in proofs for quarter eagles, threes, half eagles, eagles, and double eagles. The largest number of gold proof dollars of any year were struck in 1889, and this amounted to only 1,779 pieces. Proofs struck in all denominations per year usually ran from twenty to forty specimens. Over ten times that number or more were struck for coins in silver and copper. It is no wonder that perfect gold pieces bring very high prices today.

During the depression of 1929–33 and the uncertainty of the country's financial position, hoarding of gold coins by individuals became so common that it seriously endangered our financial structure. To end hoarding and get gold back where it could best benefit the country, the government issued an order to turn in all gold coins. The first announcement of the government order was widely publicized and stressed stiff jail sentences for failure to comply. The order accomplished what it intended, and millions of dollars in gold coins were deposited in banks and Federal Reserves.

The government was not interested in the rarity of the coins themselves, only the volume. It is therefore regrettable that, because of the hysteria of the time, many really rare gold coins were turned in. Within a few weeks, however, the original order—which exempted gold coins in quantities of no more than $100—was amended to also exempt gold coins that were considered rare and those that were held in coin collections. Over a period of years, subsequent amendments gradually continued to ease the stringency of the original order.

At first, limits were lifted on all coins but the two-and-one-half-dollar pieces; restrictions on these pieces limited ownership to not more than two of any date or mintmark. Then even this restriction was lifted, and the penalty for noncompliance was changed from a criminal to a civil one, with a fine.

Since the Hoarding Act of 1933, interest in gold-coin collecting has been growing by leaps and bounds. As soon as the government discontinued making gold coins, collectors began taking great interest in them.

There are no current restrictions regarding the export, import, purchase, sale, or possession of gold coins in the United States.

Private Gold Coins

Private territorial gold coins were issued between 1830 and 1862 in different parts of the country to answer a demand for denominations lacking in regular issues. While there were federal laws that forbade the individual states from striking gold coins, there were none forbidding private persons or private companies from doing so.

In 1787, the year before George Washington was elected President, a New York City jeweler named Ephraim Brasher applied to the state legislature for permission to strike copper coins to circulate in that state. Permission was refused, but that did not prevent Brasher from using the dies he had made. He struck his coins in gold, their intrinsic value being $16, the same as that of Spanish doubloons. His coins were known as Ephraim Brasher doubloons. The one with EB on the right wing of the eagle is one of the highest-priced coins in the world.

The years 1830–40 saw great industrial development and territorial expansion in our country. The first steam locomotive and the horse-drawn streetcar and ominbus were put into service; the Erie Canal was built and the telegraph invented.

In 1830, a treaty with Great Britain opened to American commerce the ports of the West Indies and South America; a treaty with Turkey opened the Black Sea. Around the same time, Templeton Reid, an assayer who did business near the gold mines of Lumpkin, Georgia, issued the first of his private gold coins. It is not definitely known how long his business operated or when it started, but the first coins to bear his stamp were dated 1830. The coins issued from his Georgia establishment contianed gold of a higher standard and fineness than any other ever issued by either private persons or the government. It is reasonable to assume that this is why so many were melted, resulting in their great scarcity.

Another Southerner, Christopher Bechtler ran an establishment in Rutherford County, North Carolina. The first of his coins, although undated, seem to have been struck in the early part of 1831. Around 1842 he passed his business on to his son August, who continued issuing coins until about 1852. The gold for these pieces came from North Carolina and Georgia.

When Texas was admitted to the Union, conflict over its boundaries resulted in the war with Mexico, which ended with the Treaty of Guadalupe Hidalgo in 1848. For $18,000,000 Mexico sold all of her northern territory to the United States. This territory included the region known as Arizona, California, Utah, Nevada, New Mexico, and part of Colorado.

So civilization had already pushed its way westward when the cry of "gold" came from California and resounded from coast to coast. There was a great exodus from the East; people poured into the West in droves. With the influx of prospectors, traders, merchants, and people from every walk of life, towns grew up overnight. It was the dawn of a Golden Age, and the Forty-niner was staking his claim.

The discovery of gold in California was a boon to a world suffering from a gold shortage. It changed the whole outlook of industry and commerce. Prices skyrocketed to unbelievable heights. For a while, gold dust was used by weight as a medium of exchange, but this was soon found to be cumbersome and impractical. The demand for gold coins was great, but there were no mints in the West. To ship gold dust to the East to be minted into coins was out of the question; progress overland was slow and was subject to the hazards of holdups and hostile Indians. An attempt was made by the provincial government in the Oregon Territory to establish a mint, but this failed. A private organization, the Oregon Exchange Company, started minting operations in Oregon City in 1849. A blacksmith was employed to make the necessary apparatus, and an engraver, one of the company's members, made the dies.

The Mormons, who for years had been migrating westward because they were expelled from New York, Illinois, and Nebraska, had finally settled on the shores of Great Salt Lake in Utah, while it was still Mexican territory. They started their own mint in 1849, striking coins from gold dust received from California. Their twenty-dollar gold piece was the first to be struck in this country, but the intrinsic value was found to be only between $16 and $18.

There were about fifteen private mints operating in California between 1849 and 1855, striking millions of dollars' worth of gold coins. Norris, Greig & Norris coined the first piece, a five-dollar coin, in 1849. Moffat & Company struck the first ten-dollar coin; Baldwin & Company, the first twenty; Moffat & Company, the first fifty. The fifty-dollar coin was octagonal, bearing the stamp of U.S. Assayer Augustus Humbert. F. D. Kohler & Company and Moffat & Company issued ingots stamped from gold bars. The last private-issue coins from California came from the mints of Wass, Mollitar & Company and Kellogg & Company in 1855;

15

a U.S. mint had been established in San Francisco the year before.

In 1857 a panic overtook the country, due to overcapitalization, overbuilding of railroads, rising prices, speculation, bad crops, bad state banking, and diminishing gold output. In 1857, while agitation grew among the states over the question of states' rights and the Dred Scott Decision, silver was discovered in Nevada, and two years later there was a new finding of gold. The Forty-niner rush was repeated but did not reach the same proportions as did the rush a decade before, because states' rebellion had become such a serious issue.

At this time, Colorado had three private minting firms of its own. Clark, Gruber & Company struck its first coins in 1860, and issued coins of all U.S. gold denominations except for ones and threes. In 1862, the government purchased the Clark, Gruber establishment, which was thereafter conducted as a U.S. Assay Office. The original bill called for a government mint in Denver, but this mint did not materialize until 1906.

In Georgia Gulch, John Parsons & Company, Tarryall Mines, and J. J. Conway & Company operated private mints for a limited period. Parsons issued quarter eagles and half eagles; Conway, quarter eagles, half eagles, and eagles. None of the coins bore dates, but they are said to have been struck in 1861. All are quite rare, Conway's exceedingly so.

The designs on these privately issued gold coins are varied. Some are very plain and carry only the name of the mint or minter, the date, and the denomination or weight. Others have very attractive original designs, and still others are so much like regular government coinage that to the ordinary layman they appear identical.

MORMON COINS

A number of the country's first gold coins can be traced to the Mormons. To aid the common cause, it was customary for each member of the Church of Latter-day Saints to give one-tenth of his income to the church, whether in cattle, produce, or money. In 1848, a Mormon named Thomas Rhoads made a fortune in gold at Sutter's Sawmill, California. In a display of enormous faith, he and his family then headed for Great Salt Lake, Utah, and turned *all* their gold over to Brigham Young to accelerate the progress of the Mormon people.

Since Salt Lake was fairly well supplied with gold dust, the council unanimously agreed that the time had come to convert the dust into coins. In order to accomplish this, President Young solicited the aid of John Kay and John Taylor in planning the first mint to be established in the Great Salt Lake Valley.

The patternmaking skills of John Kay were employed in working out suitable designs for the coins. After some time and difficulty, the preparations were finally completed and Kay began to melt the gold and roll it into sheets. A punching press was then used to punch out the gold discs, and a coining press then stamped the design on the discs.

Kay turned out ten-dollar pieces which were paid out at a premium of fifty cents on the piece. Whether the coins commanded a premium because of their novelty value or because they were overweight is not known. Twenty of them were charged out to Brigham Young and five to John Kay. A week later, twenty-one pieces were coined and charged out at par to Brigham Young. Production was then discontinued; the crucibles used to melt the gold had broken in the preliminary runs, and operations had to be suspended until they could be replaced.

Since the coining had stopped, the punching press was dismantled and shipped by ox team to Parowan, where it could be put to use while the new crucibles were being made. During the short time the press was in Parowan, it was used for cutting nails. In October, 1848, the press was returned to the valley.

With new crucibles in place and the mint once more ready for operation, Kay struck a few test pieces bearing a design on one side only. This time the crucibles held; and in September, 1849, the mint resumed production. The punching press returned from Parowan was used to produce the 1849–50 gold coins and later, the 1860 coinage.

The design of the gold coins minted in Salt Lake City consisted of clasped hands in the center of the obverse, with the date 1849 below; the legend reads "G.S.L.C.P.G." (Great Salt Lake City Pure Gold), "Two and half Do." On the reverse is a crown over the all-seeing eye, and around the edge, the words "HOLINESS TO THE LORD." The designs on the 1849 and 1850 coins were all the same with the exception of the 1850 five-dollar piece. This had nine stars around the edge and a slightly different crown.

The general belief is that during the early coinage no effort was made to assay or refine the gold because no one connected with the mint was capable of determining a proper standard. Captain H. Stansbury has substantiated this fact in his report on his exploration and survey of Great Salt Lake. The coinage was done in good faith, however, because of the then prevailing theory of "relative fineness"; in other words, the Mormons based the worth of all gold upon the purity of California gold. Little did they realize that although the coins minted from native gold were full weight, in assay, they were below face value or fineness of the gold. According to Colonel Lock, the 1849 five-dollar gold piece was actually worth $4.51. This mistake was later brought to light, but not before losses had been sustained by many who had purchased gold on the relative-fineness theory.

COMMEMORATIVE COINS

The opening of the Chicago World's Fair in 1892 was the occasion for the issue of the first U.S. commemorative coin, the Columbian silver half dollar. Designed to help defray expenses, it did not meet with great enthusiasm. A good many specimens were coined in 1892, and still more in 1893. It was hoped that nearly 2,500,000 of both dates could be sold at one dollar each.

Many were purchased and taken home as souvenirs of the exposition. A great many, however, did not sell and were ultimately placed in circulation at face value. For many years it was not unusual to receive one of these Columbian half dollars, particularly one dated 1893, in one's pocket change. Silver Isabella quarters also were struck in 1893, but were issued in much smaller quantities and therefore did not prove so great a disappointment as the Columbian halves.

Even though these first U.S. commemoratives did not achieve their anticipated success, a precedent was set, and the idea of raising funds by minting special-occasion coins to sell at a premium took hold. Silver commemorative issues have been appearing ever since. In 1900, we had our first commemorative dollar, the silver Washington Lafayette.

In 1903, the centennial of the Louisiana Purchase was marked by the issuance of our first gold commemorative coins, the

Jefferson and McKinley gold dollars. Other gold commemorative issues, in various denominations, have followed.

The year 1915 saw the appearance of the Panama-Pacific gold dollar, gold quarter eagle ($2.50 piece), and gold fifty-dollar coins. The fifty-dollar pieces, struck in both a round and an octagonal shape, became very rare. Though they were issued more as historical souvenirs than as coins, there was trouble disposing of them at any price over face value.

People resisted paying a premium for a coin, no matter how interesting it was or from how small an issue. Even in the late 1920s, coin dealers were more than pleased to get back their capital investment in a Panama-Pacific fifty-dollar slug plus a small premium for their efforts.

While approximately a thousand of the Panama-Pacific fifty-dollar pieces were struck of each type, nearly half of them were turned in to the mint to be melted down. This leaves a little over a thousand of both in existence today. Collectors prize a Panama-Pacific set—the two fifty-dollar gold pieces, a gold quarter eagle, and a gold dollar, the set completed by a Panama-Pacific silver half dollar.

TEDDY ROOSEVELT'S TWENTY-DOLLAR GOLD PIECE

In the winter of 1905, President Theodore Roosevelt met in Washington with the sculptor August Saint-Gaudens, whose work he had long admired. The conversation drifted to the beauty of ancient Greek coins, which Saint-Gaudens believed to be without peer in artistic merit. The President expressed his wish for the United States to issue coins that would rival the Greek ones in beauty. To this end, he commissioned Saint-Gaudens to model finer designs for new U.S. coins.

Demonstrating his versatility and extraordinary energy, President Roosevelt found the time to personally oversee a two-year endeavor to produce the new coin designs. The model finally adopted for the gold double eagle (twenty-dollar piece) was of unusually high artistic merit. The obverse presented a standing figure of Liberty, holding aloft in her right hand the torch of enlightenment and in her left, the olive branch of peace. On the reverse was a rendering of a flying eagle above a rising sun.

At the President's order, a few experimental pieces were struck with extremely high relief. These exceedingly rare pieces are easily distinguishable from the ones issued later for general circulation. While the later coins also have unusually high relief, the field of the rare experimental pieces is quite deeply concave. It connects directly with the edge without any border, giving it a sharp, knifelike appearance. Liberty's skirt shows two folds at the side of the right leg, and the Capitol building in the background at the left is very small. The date, 1907, is expressed in Roman numerals: MCMVII. The sun, on the reverse side, has fourteen rays.

In addition to these experimental pieces, 11,250 high-relief twenty-dollar gold pieces were struck on a medal press for general distribution and are found today in many collections. There is a border around the edge, Liberty's skirt has three folds at the side of the right leg, and the Capitol is considerably larger. The date, 1907, is again in Roman numerals. On the reverse, there are only thirteen rays extending from the sun.

For practical reasons, and especially since these high-relief coins 'could not be struck on a regular coin press and would not stack, the decision was soon made to revert to the customary flat relief. A large number of similar flat-relief double eagles were issued in 1907, and in later years up to 1933, when the issuance of gold coins was discontinued. These pieces show the date in Arabic numerals.

Theodore Roosevelt's personal twenty-dollar gold piece, donated by Cornelius Roosevelt, is on permanent display in the Smithsonian Institution's Hall of Monetary History. It should remind us of Roosevelt's words about this piece: "Certain things were done, of which the economic bearing was more remote but which bore directly upon our welfare, because they add to the beauty of living and therefore the joy of life."

2.
FACTORS THAT
INFLUENCE THE
PRICE OF GOLD

In contrast to numismatic coins, which are valued for their rarity, condition, and aesthetic qualities, the value of bullion coins is determined by the value of their bullion content. Thus, numismatic coins are for the collector, while bullion is for the investor, interested simply in making a profit.

Gold is becoming an increasingly accepted and viable medium of investment. Although it is impossible to say what direction gold will take in the future, there are financial signals that generally indicate when the price of gold is headed for a downward slope or an upward trend. The future of gold is influenced by the state of the economy, the rate of inflation, the value of the dollar, supply and demand, and speculation.

For gold to do well, the economy must be healthy. When the country is in a recession, the price of gold usually goes down. Conversely, when the country is experiencing economic, expansion, the price of gold goes up. Traumatic shocks on the economy, such as the record-shattering drop of the stock market on October 19, 1987, have adverse effects on coins and bullion.

The day after the crash, bullion went down sharply. As a result, people became nervous and stopped buying. When collectors resumed buying, they gravitated toward "safe" coins, avoiding any that might pose a risk. Many experts believed that the stock-market crash would lead to inflation, driving up the price of gold, but these events did not occur.

When the rate of inflation is high, people generally turn to gold as a hedge. When inflation is low, they invest elsewhere. When the dollar is strong, people place their money in dollar-denominated investments such as bonds and treasury bills. In contrast, investors panic when the dollar is weak and put their money into precious metals, causing the value of gold to go up.

Although the government and private individuals own enough gold to preclude a shortage, sporadic fluctuations in the market can cause temporary shortages which drive the price of gold up. Similarly, a temporary surplus causes the price of gold to fall. The activities of South Africa and the Soviet Union, the largest and second-largest producers of gold, can cause these market fluctuations.

In the past, South Africa has been careful in selling the precious metal, using it to support the world market price. However, economic sanctions placed on the country have forced it to sell gold as fast as it can in order to gain much-needed foreign currency. Due to the increased production of gold by many other countries, South Africa does not play the role it once did in influencing the world market.

The gold movements of the Soviet Union also have less of an effect than previously on the global marketplace. Recently, the Soviets have been cash-hungry and have been selling their gold, but this has had little effect on the price, which has remained virtually unchanged for quite awhile.

Speculators monitor fluctuations and act accordingly. If, for example, it appears that the price of gold is going to go up, they eagerly buy the metal in that expectation—in the process, pushing the price up far higher than it would have gone. Similarly, if a drop in the price of gold is predicted, they quickly sell off their gold while the price is still high, thus aggravating the descent.

Although gold spiraled upward immediately following the stock-market crash of October 1987, going as high as $537 an ounce, it went back down within two days, and eventually settled in the $360–$380 range where it has remained ever since. At first this seemed to negate the long-held theory that gold moves opposite to stocks, but in the long run stocks climbed and gold decreased.

Prior to the stock-market crash, interest rates had been rising for many months, and yields on Treasury bonds and bills moved to their highest point in years. Thus, when the stock market crashed, investors ran to higher interest rates, rather than to gold.

When correlating the price of gold with the stock market, it is important to look at the underlying economic factors that led up to the crash. By the end of 1986, the value of the dollar was at a ten-year low in relation to many European currencies, and a thirty-year low against the Japanese yen. The government was concerned that if the dollar continued to drop, the resultant higher prices for foreign products would induce domestic manufacturers to raise their own prices, and price inflation would result.

To prevent this from happening, the Federal Reserve decided to intervene and reduce the money supply, seeing that fewer dollars translate into higher value for existing dollars. Additionally, it was hoped that a stronger dollar would reduce our trade deficit. By the summer of 1987, the growth of the money supply dropped almost to zero. To further combat inflation, interest rates were pushed higher.

Less cash and higher interest rates had the intended effect overseas, resulting in a stronger dollar. However, while all eyes were focused on the dollar, no one was watching Wall Street. In October the trade figures came in, and instead of showing a decline in the U.S. trade deficit they showed an increase. The day after these figures were released, the stock market plunged 200 points, and shortly thereafter, 500 points.

Immediately after the drop, the Federal Reserve reversed its policy, and increased the money supply while lowering interest rates. While this should have resulted in an immediate decline in the value of the dollar, the Federal Reserve prevented that by also supporting the dollar, buying approximately half a billion dollars on foreign exchange markets in less than a week. This provided temporary stabilization.

Few people were pacified, however. The dollar's rise was obviously caused by government intervention, and everyone waited to see what it would do on its own when the government stopped supporting it. Two weeks later, the government stopped intervening and the dollar plunged, leading the way into recession.

A recession will normally slow down inflation, which in turn will hold down the price of gold. Gold is looked upon by most investors as a hedge against inflation. With no inflation and no immediate signs of a coming inflation, gold prices have remained flat. Ironically, low interest rates make gold easier to buy at a time when there is not much interest.

Investors make up 50 percent of the gold market—jewelry accounts for nearly the entire other half. In a recession, consumers tend to have less disposable cash for items such as jewelry. This is another reason for gold's flat price. As the country comes out of its recession, be on the lookout for inflation and a rise in the price of gold.

HISTORY OF GOLD PRICES

Now that we have discussed factors that influence the future price of gold, we may want to examine what influenced prices in the past. In the year 1250, gold was valued at the equivalent of a modest $4.50 an ounce. It took centuries for the price to reach $25 an ounce—in sharp contrast to today's market, in which the price of gold can change more than $25 in less than an hour.

The reason for this long period of stability was that governments controlled the price of gold and kept it artificially within limits.

In 1250, European nations began to mint new gold coins to use to trade with the Byzantine Empire. Gold was used in trade because of its stability. By the late 1280s, every major nation issued gold coins except England, which used the pound sterling. England finally turned to gold coinage under Edward III (1327 to 1377).

During this same period, the price of gold rose to $6.75 per ounce. Marginal increases followed until it reached $10 an ounce in 1492, the year of Columbus' epoch-making first voyage.

In the 1500s, gold was brought to Europe from the New World in such tremendous volume that it unbalanced the European economic structure. In England, for example, prices subsequently rose by 100 percent while wages rose only 20 percent.

In the United States, the adoption of the gold standard in 1792 specified the official price of gold as $19.393939 an ounce. The value was revised in 1834 to $20.68965517, and in 1837 it was slightly decreased to $20.67183462; there it remained unchanged until the depression of 1933.

The Napoleonic wars in the early 1800s affected gold prices in Europe. Napoleon made money from his wars, and after every victory hoarded gold francs in preparation for the next campaign, thus driving up the price.

In 1865, a small number of European countries formed the Latin Monetary Union, standardizing the fineness, weight, size, and denomination of the gold coins issued by its members. The group based the value of gold on a silver:gold ratio of 15½:1. This bimetallic standard caused silver to fall on the world market, and silver coins of many countries became debased. On the principle of Gresham's Law, "bad money drives out good money," the falling value of silver also threatened the future of gold coins. There was the distinct possibility that they could be driven out of circulation. Eventually, in 1927, the Union was disbanded. We have as a positive legacy that some of the gold coins were struck in large enough numbers that they are still available to collectors today.

3.
STARTING A
COIN COLLECTION

When purchasing gold coins, there are a number of steps the consumer should follow. Like any other commodity, gold coins are an investment, and as such require careful consideration before one commits large sums of money.

KNOW YOUR DEALER

The single most important step is to know your dealer. Among the great many dealers in the gold-coin market, some are reputable and some are not. Therefore, it is imperative to do a little research before selecting a dealer. One should ask other collectors what they know about the particular dealer, and check with the local Better Business Bureau or Chamber of Commerce to see if there are any outstanding complaints against him.

Unfortunately, Better Business Bureau reports cover only the previous three-year period. A more thorough investigation would entail inquiries to your state's attorney general and the Federal Trade Commission. It is also valuable to find out how many years the dealer has operated under the same name and what other names, if any, he has used. This will ensure against selecting a dealer who might have been convicted of a felony or who has changed his company's name or location a number of times. A dealer who had demonstrated stability is preferable to one who has not.

Once you have determined that the dealer does not have a questionable past, make certain that he provides a guarantee of authenticity and maintains a return policy. A good dealer will guarantee a coin in writing, and promise to refund the purchase price if the coin is later found to be counterfeit or to have been altered in any way. Additionally, ask if he allows prospective buyers to send coins to a certification service (see page xx) to confirm their grading. The Sheldon numerical grading system is widely employed. Many dealers however, use different grading systems. When purchasing a coin it is advisable to have the dealer state in writing which grading system he is using. Below is a general trading table with which the buyer should be familiar:

GRADING TABLE

Proof (PR.) .... A coin with a mirrorlike image struck specifically for collectors.
Proof-like (P.L.) .... An uncirculated coin with an extremely sharp image which resembles that of a proof.
Uncirculated (UNC) .... A regular mint issue that was never put into circulation.
Almost Uncirculated (A.U.).. A coin showing minimal wear.
Extremely Fine (EX.FINE).. A slightly circulated coin that shows very little evidence of wear and has retained much of its luster.
Very Fine (V.FINE) .... Shows noticeable wear on high spots, but still displays some luster.
Fine (F) .... Obviously circulated, but the letters and mottos remain clear and bold.
Very Good (V.G.)........... The features are still clear and sharp.
Good (G)................. The features are clear, but not sharp.
Fair (FAIR)............... Displays of excessive wear, though features can still be identified.

Many collectors tend to judge a dealer on the basis of his professional affiliations. This is not an adequate criterion, since most associations admit anyone willing to pay the fees. There are a few associations such as the Professional Numisimatists Guild (PNG) who admit only members approved by a majority of the dealers in the country. Still, the buyer should remember that even these organizations may include dishonorable dealers.

TYPES OF DEALERS

In addition to evaluating reputability, the beginning coin collector should be aware of the different types of dealers.

Local Coin Shops. Local coin shops are an excellent place for a new buyer to acquire practical knowledge about coins. These shops stock collector paraphernalia such as reference books and coin holders, as well as inexpensive coins. They do not, however, maintain large inventories of expensive or rare coins. Consequently, as one acquires more knowledge and expertise it might become necessary to find a larger dealer.

Regional Dealers. Regional dealers are very good sources for the beginning buyer. These are medium-sized to large firms which serve collectors throughout a large, regionally based area. They maintain a large inventory consisting of bullion coins for the investor as well as numismatic coins for the collector. Their prices are very competitive, because they tend to have low overhead and a fast turnover of inventory. In addition, these firms employ numismatists, giving the new buyer the opportunity to speak with an expert.

"Mega-Dealers." Mega-dealers are the largest rare-coin firms. They maintain large inventories in which more often than not can be found a number of very valuable coins. These firms usually employ a large number of specialists who attend many coin shows and auctions, where they are able to purchase large quantities of coins. The only disadvantage in dealing with this type of firm is that it is difficult to establish a one-to-one relationship with one of the numismatists. Additionally, mega-dealers have high overhead, and consequently usually charge higher prices.

Quasi-Numismatic Dealers. It is a good idea for the beginning collector to avoid "quasi-numismatic" dealers, such as antiques shops, jewelry dealers, pawnbrokers, and others who do not deal primarily in coins. owners and employees of these firms are probably not numismatists and may be unfamiliar with grading and authenticity. More than likely they also will not guarantee their coins. The more advanced collector might sometimes find excellent deals at such places, since the "quasi-numismatic" may be unaware of the rarity of some coins and will often undervalue them.

Auctions. Auctions are an excellent source for rare and high-quality coins. However, they are not a good place for a beginner who is unfamiliar with coins, because it is impossible to bid on a coin without knowing what it is worth.

After deciding on dealers to do business with, it is valuable to cultivate good relationships with them. Dealers are less likely to overgrade or overprice a coin if they have a close relationship with the buyer. One should avoid dealers who are too "busy" to answer questions or to take the time to educate potential and established customers.

KNOW THE MARKETPLACE

In addition to knowing the dealer, it is imperative that before purchasing any coin, one know the marketplace and have a basic knowledge of grading techniques. There are many books and videos available which are excellent sources for the beginning collector. *A Guide Book of United States Coins* (the red book), by R. S. Yeoman, is generally considered the bible of the coin industry, and is a good place to begin familiarizing oneself with coins and prices.

Computer owners will definitely want to purchase a program called COINS/PLUS. In addition to supplying a database with coin prices regularly updated, this excellent program provides a way to inventory your collection for tax and insurance purposes. It also supplies a "want-list" feature to track prices on future purchases. COINS/PLUS is sold by Compu-Quote, 6914 Berquist Avenue, Canoga Park, California 91307. Phone: (800) 782-6775; in California: (818) 348-3662.

For those who prefer visual stimulation, there are two excellent videos on the market, "Collecting and Grading U.S. Coins" and "Coins: Genuine, Counterfeit & Altered," both produced by Educational Video Inc., 31800 Plymouth Road, Livonia, Michigan 48150. A good reference library is a small investment compared with the thousands of dollars that are often spent haphazardly purchasing coins.

When one is ready to begin buying coins, it is advisable to avoid the common ones. Many mass marketers will promote a common coin claiming it has the potential to increase substantially in value. This is generally untrue; coins that are common now are likely to remain so in the future. It should be noted, however, that even though a coin is common enough to be promoted, it may still be scarce enough to be considered an investment. For example, Saint-Gaudens double eagles are considered scarce; however, they have universal appeal to investors and therefore are highly promoted. These should be purchased only from a reputable dealer and should be confirmed by an independent certification organization for grade and authenticity. The best investments are high-quality coins and those which are scarce or rare. Historically, these tend to increase the most in value.

CERTIFICATION SERVICES

It is advisable to become familiar with the idiosyncrasies of the various certification services. There is no uniform standard for grading coins, and some services tend to be more conservative than others. The strict grading services are the American Numismatic Association Certification Service (ANACS), the Professional Coin Grading Service (PCGS), and the Numismatic Guaranty Corporation of America (NGC).

DETERMINING THE QUALITY OF COINS

Before purchasing coins, one should learn how to recognize high quality. Coins that have maintained the highest levels of preservation appreciate most quickly. Collectors unfamiliar with the various gradations of coin quality will often pay the price of a coin in superior condition for a specimen that is just average.

A Fine coin is one that shows a reasonable amount of wear but is still desirable. The basic outline is clear, but much of the fine detail is worn away. All lettering should be legible. The next grade below this is Very Good, a considerably worn but not altogether unattractive coin. A coin in this condition should be free of serious gouges or other mutilations, but it may be somewhat scratched from use. Numismatically, a coin rated only Good is a minimum-condition coin. The date and mint mark are legible and the major portions of the design distinguishable. Fair indicates a badly worn coin that is usually not acceptable to a collector. A Fair coin is generally used only as a space filler until a better coin can be acquired.

The grade above Fine is Very Fine, a coin on which the design is still quite clean, and which overall shows the very slightest amount of wear. An Extremely Fine coin shows the slightest signs of wear or rubbing only on the very highest points of the design. Uncirculated indicates a coin absolutely without wear. Above Uncirculated is Proof—a special coin with a mirror-like surface minted especially for collectors. The Proof coin must be absolutely perfect.

The three most important qualities to look for are toning, luster, and strike. Look for types of toning that make a coin attractive, avoiding those which appear corroded or tarnished. Additionally, look for a coin with a smooth surface that reflects light and is free of imperfections.

Accurate classification of the condition of a coin is extremely important. For the beginning coin collector, this exacting work should be mastered first. The novice may risk losing a good amount of money by paying high prices for coins or coin collections that are grossly overrated. If when buying coins you have any doubt whatever as to whether a certain piece is in the condition represented, take it to an expert or another experienced collector. He will gladly give you an opinion free of charge. When purchasing a large collection, don't hesitate to have a dealer appraise it for you and give you his written expert opinion. The fee you pay for an expert appraisal may save you many hundreds of dollars in the long run.

With the values of uncirculated coins steadily increasing, it is essential that the serious collector know how to determine whether or not a coin is actually uncirculated. Some of the cleaning processes used today make it necessary to apply very careful examination. While many cleaned coins look like uncirculated pieces, closer scrutiny will show they have some wear.

If properly cleaned, truly uncirculated pieces are not decreased in value, though under some circumstances it is preferable to have them in their natural state. Too frequently, we look at a coin and because it appears bright and new, consider it uncirculated. The actual wear on such a piece should be the determining factor in our decision to invest.

COUNTERFEIT COINS

The rapid rise in price of U.S. gold coins has created a flood of counterfeits, altered dates, and other kind of forgeries, many of which are so clever that the best experts are sometimes fooled. Watch out for the following:

Twenty-dollar gold pieces. All U.S. twenties are being coined, with the proper amount of gold, in foreign countries, designed to be sold to American collectors. If you examine the feathers in the center of the eagle on the reverse, you will find them too sharply tooled. These coins also have a very proof-like, mirror-type surface. Beware of Liberty Heads of rare dates that have no mintmark and thus appear to be from the Philadelphia Mint. There are common coins from branch mints whose mintmarks have been cleverly removed. Foreign-made counterfeit Liberty Heads have very sharp milling and appear too new for their dates.

Ten-dollar gold pieces. Watch out for the 1858P; it is known to exist with the mintmark of a branch mint removed. All tens are being coined in Europe at present.

Five-dollar gold pieces. Also watch out for the 1909O, as the O mintmark is known to have been added. All fives are being counterfeited.

Four-dollar stellas. Beware of patterns struck in inferior metals, gold-plated, and being sold as gold stellas. The 1880 series coins are presently being struck in Europe.

Three-dollar gold pieces. It is possible that the later dates are being struck in Europe. They have a mirror-like appearance.

Quarter-eagles ($2.50 pieces). Both types, Indian Head and Liberty Head, are being struck in large quantities in Europe. They have the correct weight in gold and are very nearly perfect.

On fake Liberty Heads the head stands out too sharply, the edge of the coin is a trifle flat, and the milling is too sharp. These have a granular surface, and they come in many dates. As for the Indian Heads, it is difficult to tell, but there again the milling is too fine and sharp.

Gold dollars. Coins of pretty nearly every date and mint have been copied. These, for the most part, have a granular surface; the beading on the edge tends to be too flat, the milling much too sharp; the deep-cut work "Liberty" on the headdress is usually sharp in the center and weak toward the end of the word. These are the new counterfeits struck in Europe. They are very dangerous because they are of the correct weight and fineness of gold. Old counterfeits are very easy to detect because the gold content is inferior. The very rare 1854C has been faked by the addition of a sweated letter C to the date. Mintmarks also are known to have been sweated to imitate nearly all of the rarer branch-mint gold dollars. In all denominations, these new European gold counterfeits are made by the centrifugal molding process and are very cleverly done.

CLEANING COINS

Originally, the cleaning of coins was taboo. Early cleaning practices attempted to make the cleaned coins look as much as possible as if they had not been cleaned. Today, however, well-cleaned coins are accepted as readily as—and sometimes more readily than—those which have been kept in their original state, although there are some exceptions. The value of the coins and the technique used in cleaning are both factors in the coin's desirability.

Never clean any badly worn coin. It is a waste of time, and cleaning a coin that is in less than Very Fine condition will never enhance it.

Proofs in gold will seldom if ever need cleaning. Additionally, gold Uncirculated coins and Very Fine and Extremely Fine gold coins do not need to be cleaned very often. If it becomes absolutely necessary to clean them, wash them gently with Ivory soap and warm water.

4.

BULLION COINS
FOR THE INVESTOR

The 1985 ban on the sale of South Africa Krugerrands in the United States has been offset by American production of gold coins primarily for sale to investors.

In the fall of 1986, the government issued the American Eagle, a legal-tender one-ounce gold coin whose price is pegged to the value of gold. Also issued were three fractional bullion gold coins, containing one-half, one-fourth, and one-tenth of an ounce of gold. These coins are the first in the history of the United States to be sold specifically for investment purposes. As such, they have been an unqualified success.

The American Eagle program encountered controversy from the day the idea was conceived. Opponents argued that the market was already too saturated for a new coin to gain a competitive place in the gold market. Although gold coins from South Africa were banned, a range of other alternatives still existed, such as the Canadian Maple Leaf and the Chinese Panda, both of which have gained immense popularity. The American Eagles were created not to fill a void left by the ban on Krugerrands, but rather as an attempt to gain a share of a large and growing market dominated in recent history by other countries.

The American Eagle coins would offer both an old design and a new one. The obverse of the gold coin displays a modified figure of Liberty inspired by the Saint-Gaudens design for the 1907 double eagle. The reverse presents A Family of Eagles, an original design created by a Dallas artist, Mrs. Miley Busiek. This design was intended as a tribute to American family life.

The American Eagles were an instant success. Demand was so great that supplies grew short or nonexistent, and prices rose well above normal levels for bullion coins. These soon were the best-selling bullion coins in the world. As U.S. supplies ran out, many investors bought them on overseas markets, paying exorbitant sums well above their bullion value.

The problem stemmed in part from the fact that officials assumed the one-ounce American Eagle would be more in demand than the fractional pieces. Consequently, the U.S. Mint did not produce as many fractionals, resulting in runaway situations with the half-, quarter-, and tenth-of-an-ounce Eagles. Until more were issued, market pressures pushed their prices well above their bullion worth.

According to official mintage figures, the coinage in 1986 was 1,363,000 one-ounce Eagles, 620,000 half-ounce Eagles, 751,000 quarter-ounce Eagles, and 913,000 tenth-ounce Eagles.

Although many more have since been issued, the 1986 Eagles command 20 to 30 percent more than the later coins, simply because fewer were minted.

The success of the American Eagles has been a boon for the gold market as a whole. The Eagle program brought many new investors into the market. Now that the U.S. Government is issuing bullion coins, gold has gained wider general respectability among investment-minded Americans.

The American Arts Gold Medallions, issued in 1978 as the first U.S. attempt to enter the world gold bullion market, did not fare as well as the American Eagles. The coins were a dismal failure and were terminated in December of 1985.

The first coins of the issue came off the press in July of 1980. Artist Grant Wood, known for his painting *American Gothic,* was depicted on the one-ounce, and singer Marian Anderson on the half-ounce. The 1981 issue depicted Mark Twain and Willa Cather; 1982 issues, Louis Armstrong and Frank Lloyd Wright; 1983 Robert Frost and Alexander Calder; and 1984 John Steinbeck and Helen Hayes. The only ones that did nominally well were the Frank Lloyd Wright half-ounce issue of 1982 and the Robert Frost one-ounce piece of 1983.

The problem with the medallions was that they tended to be regarded as collector's items rather than as bullion investments, as originally intended. Consequently they were no competition for the Krugerrand or Canadian Maple Leaf.

GOLD ON A BUDGET

For the collector, investing in gold does not require a substantial amount of money. In addition to the American Eagle fractional gold coins, seven other types of U.S. gold coins can be obtained for about $300 in Extremely Fine or even Uncirculated condition. These are the Types I and III gold dollar; the Liberty quarter eagle ($2.50), half eagle ($5), and eagle ($10); and the Indian quarter eagle and stella ($4) coins.

Since so much recent emphasis has been on the American Eagles, prices for these coins have remained low. A collector who can set aside $50 to $100 a month should be able to assemble an American gold-type set.

The Indian half eagle, which has always been considered a popular coin, can be purchased for $300 or less. For those who prefer underrated coins, the Liberty quarter eagle is a good buy. With the Indian quarter eagle and the Liberty half eagle, there is virtually no difference in price between a low-grade coin and an Almost Uncirculated specimen.

For those willing to spend a little more, eagle and double eagle ($20) gold coins can be purchased for about $600. A high-grade Saint-Gaudens, considered to be the most beautiful coin issued by the United States, is only around $600 for one of the later mintage dates.

Another good buy are the Coronet-type double eagles, which are available for $500. A $20 gold coin contains almost a full ounce of gold, making it almost a no-lose proposition.

It is also possible to put together a relatively inexpensive gold collection by purchasing coins with regional accents. California, Texas, and South Dakota all have state-produced bullion pieces.

Modern California gold pieces have been in existence since late 1984. Rarities Mint of Anaheim, California, produces pure-gold bullion coins of one ounce, one-half ounce, one-quarter ounce, and one-tenth ounce. Once these gold pieces were declared exempt from state sales tax, they began to compete successfully with foreign products such as the Chinese Panda and Canadian Maple Leaf. Initial sales of the California coins totaled 2,500 ounces in a nine-month period. Sales reached this figure in only three weeks after the coins were declared exempt from state taxes.

The California brown bear is shown on the obverse, while the Great Seal of the State of California appears on the reverse. The 1986 issues have slight modifications: the bear is bolder-looking while the stars surrounding the bear are more three-dimensional.

The Rarities Mint marks all the coins with serial numbers and provides certificates of authenticity guaranteeing the purity and weight of the gold. Unlike U.S. bullion coins, which have a fineness of .917, these are pure gold. The State of California receives a $4 royalty on each ounce sold.

Colonial Coins in Houston, Texas, began minting one-ounce gold coins the year of the Texas Independence Sesquicentennial. Since then it has begun also producing fractional denominations. Both faces of the coins present the Great Seal of the State of Texas. Profits from the sale of Texas bullion go to Texas tourism and the Texas Historical Society.

South Dakota got into the act and began minting limited editions of five-ounce and one-ounce gold bullion pieces. The obverse features the Great Seal of the State of South Dakota, while the reverse displays a design selected in a statewide contest. A percentage of the profits goes toward construction of the Dakota Heritage Center, which contains state historical memorabilia.

Although collecting gold coins requires a higher investment than collecting those in other metals, there are many advantages:

1. There are fewer varieties of gold coins than there are of silver or bronze, making it possible to assemble an unusual and valuable collection with a smaller number of coins.

2. Gold coins were originally minted in quantities much smaller than silver or bronze. Additionally, gold coins were frequently melted down, making surviving coins far scarcer and thus more valuable.

3. In the past, gold coins were often hoarded and seldom circulated on a wide basis. Consequently, the collector can obtain many varieties as Proof, Proof-like, or Uncirculated specimens.

4. Gold is historically considered the ultimate standard of value.

5. A gold coin has a much higher intrinsic value than a coin of silver or copper. When the dollar is devalued, the intrinsic value of a gold coin rises.

6. Gold coins have aesthetic appeal because of their color and their artistic designs.

7. Gold coins are very marketable and can be liquidated almost immediately.

8. Gold coins are immune to the detrimental effects of oxygen and age, and do not tarnish or corrode; they can therefore be stored more easily than silver or copper.

9. Since many people regard gold merely as a source of bullion, rare coins can occasionally be bought for bargain prices.

10. The history of gold as a standard of intrinsic value, as well as gold coins' numismatic value, spans more than twenty-five centuries, ensuring that it is likely to continue as a viable investment.

These ten points not only indicate that gold is one of the best metals for investment, but also demonstrate the dual nature of gold coins. They have intrinsic value which attracts the investor, and numismatic value which attracts the collector.

5.
COMMEMORATIVE COINS
FOR THE COLLECTOR

In the past few years, U.S. commemorative coins have been among the world's best-selling and most profitable gold coins. These include ten-dollar 1984 Olympic commemoratives, five-dollar Statue of Liberty commemoratives, and five-dollar Bicentennial of the Constitution coins; and in addition to these, there is a five-dollar 1988 Olympic gold coin.

In anticipation of the 1984 Olympic Games, Congress authorized production of a ten-dollar gold piece to commemorate and help finance that year's Summer Olympics in Los Angeles. Much thought and deliberation went into the design of the coin, which was to be the nation's first new gold piece in more than fifty years. John Mercanti, a talented engraver at the Philadelphia Mint, took the basic concept of an Olympic eagle and produced a final design of remarkable craftsmanship.

Coins of this design were struck with mintmarks from West Point, Philadelphia, San Francisco, and Denver. All the pieces struck were Proof except for 75,886 specimens minted at West Point to be sold as Uncirculated coins. Philadelphia had the lowest production level, producing 33,309 pieces, while San Francisco and Denver production levels were slightly under 50,000. The Proof ten-dollar coin from West Point was the most heavily produced, with over 381,000 pieces minted. The total number of 1984 Olympic coins produced is quite small in comparison with other coinages, and they are considered an excellent buy in terms of potential for appreciation; their value is already far in excess of their issue price.

Immediately following the success of the Olympic gold coins, the United States produced the five-dollar Statue of Liberty commemorative gold coin, whose proceeds were to help finance restoration work on the statue and on Ellis Island. Issued in relatively modest numbers, the Statue of Liberty coin was expected to do well—but no one anticipated success on the scale that occurred. The entire issue sold out after one round of orders, in response to a single solicitation addressed to regular customers on the U.S. Mint's mailing list.

The total number of coins ordered before the December 31, 1985, deadline exceeded the authorized mintage, and the government was forced to turn away many early orders. The rejection process was random, without reference to the dates on which the orders had been received. This element of suspense enhanced the allure of the coins that much more.

There are two versions of the Statue of Liberty commemorative coin—proof and uncirculated. The proof piece is the more appealing aesthetically; the uncirculated version, however, had a far lower mintage, which could make it more valuable in the long run. The U.S. Bullion Depository in West Point, New York, produced 400,000 proofs and only 100,000 coins to be offered as uncirculated.

Sold by the government for less than $200, the Statue of Liberty commemoratives immediately tripled in price. It is estimated that within a few more years, they may bring $1,000 to $1,500 apiece, and possibly more. Anyone who purchased the coin at the issue price and held on to it has bought the best investment in modern-issue coinage, and possibly one of the better investments in all of numismatics.

In 1987, the United States issued another commemorative coin—the five-dollar gold piece marking the bicentennial of the U.S. Constitution. The obverse of the coin displays a modernistic, highly stylized eagle clutching a large quill pen in its claws. A series of rays emanating from the eagle contain the motto "Liberty." The reverse shows another large quill pen in an upright position, dividing the coin in half. Superimposed on the quill are the words "We the People" in fancy script. To the left of the pen are nine stars, representing the first nine states to ratify the Constitution; to the right are four more stars which represent the rest of the thirteen original states.

Early orders were very strong for these coins, which were issued in proof and uncirculated versions. They did not, however, reach the authorized production limit of 1,000,000 coins. Orders are, in fact, still being accepted, with sales to date of approximately 800,000. Because it did not sell out, the future of this coin is questionable. Presently, those who have attempted to sell their coins have been lucky to get back the price they paid for them.

The United States issued another gold coin to commemorate its participation in the 1988 Olympic Games and to help finance U.S. Olympic teams. Although the 1984 Olympic coins were received with overwhelming enthusiasm, buyers were more skeptical about the 1988 coins. Reasons for this skepticism include the fact that the 1988 games did not take place in this country as the 1984 games did, and the two countries who hosted the games—Canada and South Korea—produced coins of their own. All of these factors raise questions about the future of the U.S. Olympic coin program.

First, it is uncertain whether collectors will purchase the coins in sufficient quantities to make the program a success, although if the coins are well received, the U.S. Olympic Committee stands to gain tens of millions of dollars from the proceeds.

In addition to the commercial outlook, there are questions of propriety which have major implications for the future of U.S. commemorative coins. The first question is whether it is appropriate for the United States to issue coins to mark an event halfway around the world. This leads to another question: will coin collectors be called upon to subsidize the Olympics every four years regardless of where the Games are held? And next, the question whether this type of program reduces commemorative coins to little more than fund-raising tokens. Also in question is the matter of the United States competing with the coin programs of the host countries, possibly undercutting their sales which are needed to finance the Games.

These issues have met with mixed response within the coin industry, even dividing the Society for U.S. Commemorative Coins, a national organization dedicated to the study and appreciation of these coins. For those who consider coin collecting a viable venture, the issues raised pose serious questions as to the future direction of commemorative coins.

6.
PROOF COINS

Proof coins are pieces struck with special care to produce perfect specimens. Proofs currently are struck at San Francisco, and bear the "S" mintmark on the obverse. Until recently they were struck by hand to ensure perfection. At all times the dies used were polished, as were the planchets. This gives the coins their mirror-like finish.

A genuine Proof must be perfect. Its field, including the tiny spaces between letters and designs, must have a mirror-like brilliance, with the designs standing out dramatically against the background. The edges are usually sharp, and the coin is perfectly centered. Sandblast or mat proofs have all these qualities except for the mirror-like finish; their field has a velvety surface instead. Proof coins, whether they are of gold, silver, or copper, are truly beautiful coins.

While the first regularly recognized issue of proofs for collectors commenced in 1858, proofs had been coined before that time. The earliest proofs were trial or experimental pieces, to test designs and dies. Very few were struck, and consequently they are now very rare. These coins were not originally offered for sale to collectors; they were treated more as presentation pieces, samples of coinage, and so forth.

In 1858, when proofs were first offered for sale to collectors, the number struck was very small. Although records of proof coinages prior to 1877 are spotty, from what information we have we can tell that the quantities were limited. By examining the records one can see how the interest in proof coins steadily increased as the years went by, their popularity centering on the lower denominations.

During the nineteenth century, proof sets were offered as minor sets, complete sets, and those with gold. The minor sets, consisting of key pieces only, were by far the most popular; second in popularity were the complete sets, containing every denomination issued in a given year. Gold coins were not very popular in proof, even though their premium cost was very little above the face value. This was due perhaps to the initial face-value investment involved. The coinage of proof double eagles ranged from only 20 to 158 proofs per year from 1865 to 1907. No proofs were minted between 1915 and 1936. The maximum number of proofs struck in 1915 for any denomination was about 1,000. In 1936, mintage of proof sets was about 3,300. This was quite an increase, but nothing like what occurred from 1936 to 1957, when 1,000,000 or so proof sets were coined.

From 1936 through 1942, proofs were not sold as sets only, as they are today. Once could purchase any quantity of any denomination to make individually selected sets. Proofs have been sold only as sets from 1950 on.

Many early strikes of regular-issue coins appear to be proofs, as the new die frequently give the coins a very bright surface. This is often true with branch-mint coins, even though no proofs have ever been struck at any of the branch mints. It can be very difficult to tell these early strikes from proof coins. However, they do not have the sharp, well-struck edges of a genuine proof. Also, the highlights are usually not sharp and the coin is not perfectly centered.

One frequently comes across attempts to fake proofs. Buffing will give an uncirculated coin a mirror-like finish, but this can usually be detected because the designs have this finish as well as the field. Even coins done more carefully, so that the designs are not buffed, can be detected by examination of the tiny surfaces between the letters and designs into which a buffer cannot reach. Of course, the sharp edges of a genuine proof are also lacking on such coins.

The uncirculated gold coins that most frequently pass for proof coins are gold dollars, particularly from the 1880s, and some of the later three-dollar gold pieces. Gold two-and-one-half, five-, ten-, and twenty-dollar pieces are also sometimes found with proof-like luster, but are usually somewhat scratched, indicating contact with other coins.

Proof sets are generally priced at fifty to seventy percent above the gold content of the coins. The fact that they are from limited mintages makes them desirable collector's items. They are *not,* however, a recommended purchase as investor items. Proof sets often, in fact, are bad investments. Because one pays a premium for them, there is just as good a chance that the value will go down to below the issue price as there is that it will go above it. And this can be true even with very low mintages.

A further concern to the buyer is the proliferation of proof sets in recent years. With the vast choice of sets available it is necessary to consider what will keep interest high in a particular set. Newer Olympic coin series for example, may renew interest in the old 1984 Olympic proof set. A renewal of a set generally creates a demand for its predecessors. Consequently, the collector should look at a series in terms of what its public exposure will be ten years from now, and the potential for there being a perennial demand. This is of particular importance as buyers becomes more selective in light of the overwhelming number of selections available.

Another problem with proofs is that when first issued, they may be viewed as a "hot" item. Great initial popularity can boost their value. However, when they are no longer considered "hot," they will have to be judged on their own merits. Once the initial glory dies down, the only certain value of proofs is their bullion value. This means a loss for those who paid high premium values.

One can look to the American Eagle proofs as an example. American Eagles were the sensation of 1986, with proof orders approximating 450,000 coins. In 1987, however, these coins did not fare as well. The first problem surfaced with the one-ounce gold proof coin. When the coin was first issued at $550, many thought it a risky investment. This judgment turned out to be correct; the value dropped below its issue price and has remained down. Consequently, in 1987 only 140,000 of the coins were purchased, making the bottom line for gold proofs in 1987 only half of what it was in 1986.

Because of the low order levels, many hoped the 1987 coins would eventually increase in value. To date, however, there has been little upward mobility.

7.
INVESTING IN
OLD GOLD COINS

Old U.S. gold coins are generally the least risky investment and a good area of specialization for the beginning collector. Because of these coins' numismatic value, they are not affected by sudden downward movements in the price of bullion. Thus one can safely invest in them without worrying about whether gold is on the rise or not.

The U.S. gold coins the typical collector will encounter most often, and should thus become familiar with, are as follows:

$20	double eagle, Liberty Head	1849–1907
$20	double eagle, Saint-Gaudens type	1907–1932
$10	eagle, Liberty Head	1838–1907
$10	eagle, Indian Head	1907–1933
$ 5	half eagle, Liberty Head	1839–1908
$ 5	half eagle, Indian Head	1908–1929
$ 2.50	quarter eagle, Liberty Head	1840–1907
$ 2.50	quarter eagle, Indian Head	1908–1929
$ 1	gold dollar, Liberty Head	1849–1854
$ 1	gold dollar, Indian Head	1854–1889

It is a good idea for the novice collector to begin by concentrating on one or two specific series he finds to be of interest. This allows one to become a specialist in a particular area, rather than randomly purchasing a variety of coins about which one may know nothing. By becoming an expert one is also assured of getting the best value when purchasing rare coins.

In addition, specialized collections are in greater demand than random accumulations, and are thus easier to sell. Dealers will often pay a premium price for specialized collections, and auction houses will sometimes lower their commission rates to attract them.

Assembling such a collection requires a substantial amount of money. Experts advise that no more than 15 percent of an individual's total net worth (excluding the value of his residence) should be invested in rare coins. It is thus advisable to set a goal and then make purchases accordingly. Many collectors begin by assembling eight-piece sets which contain examples of the Liberty Head and the Indian Head quarter eagles, the Liberty Head and the Indian Head half eagles, the Liberty Head and the Indian Head eagles, and the Liberty Head and the Saint-Gaudens double eagles. A set such as this is easy to complete and relatively inexpensive. Any number of other types of sets can be created with little difficulty. For example, one could assemble a set to focus on a specific denomination, or a set of specimens of all the types of gold coins issued by the United States during a particular time span.

Many collectors prefer to concentrate on coins issued by particular mints. Each of the six branch mints is designated by a small identifying initial, usually on the reverse. Coins struck at the main mint in Philadelphia are unmarked. The initials for the branch mints are as follows:

C—Charlotte, North Carolina	(1838–1861)
CC—Carson City, Nevada	(1870–1893)
D—Dahlonega, Georgia	(1838–1861)
D—Denver, Colorado	(after 1906)
O—New Orleans, Louisiana	(1838–1909)
S—San Francisco, California	(after 1854)

The most popular specimens are those struck at Carson City, Dahlonega, and Charlotte. As it is quite difficult and expensive to acquire an entire set from one of these mints, it is a good idea to concentrate on one specific denomination. For example, one might focus on Dahlonega quarter eagles.

Mintmarks are very important to some collectors, since branch mints issue fewer coins than Philadelphia. Nevertheless, it is not advisable to pay a high premium for a coin solely because of its rare mintmark. This type of numismatic value is the most prone to reconsideration and downward adjustment; there is a high risk in paying premium prices for rare mintmarks on otherwise common coins. It is safer to pay more for rare dates or types.

Many collectors prefer to focus on a particular series of coins.

This is more difficult than other methods because many series contain extremely rare and high-priced coins. The easiest series to assemble is the Indian Head quarter eagles, which were produced from 1908 until 1929. All of the dates are easy to come by in all grades except Gem Uncirculated. Additionally, only one date in the series, the 1911-D, sells for a premium. Other popular series are the Indian Head half eagles and the Saint-Gaudens double eagles. These take a little more time and patience to collect because they contain a number of very rare dates. This means, of course, that they will also require a higher budget.

A more complex and involved method is collecting by condition and rarity. This method involves purchasing coins that are of unusually high grades in their respective issues. Researchers have compiled a "Condition Census" for the older issues, detailing the five or so coins of the highest quality for a specific issue. This can be done with a relatively high degree of accuracy for rare coins such as the 1865-S eagle; it is nearly impossible, however, to do for common coins.

Collectors with a high budget often prefer to concentrate on "exotic" coins. These are coins struck prior to 1834. Although these coins are expensive in relation to more recent issues, experts feel they are currently undervalued. For example, Attractive Very Fine and Extremely Fine half eagles of the 1798–1813 era can be purchased for as little as $1,500–$3,000, while eagles from the 1798–1803 era can be purchased in similar grades for $2,500–$4,250 per coin.

There are several ways to go about purchasing old U.S. coins. Because of the presence on the market of many authentic-looking counterfeits, it is advisable to buy through a reputable dealer who is also a specialist. Auctions are good places to purchase rare gold coins, because many rare pieces seldom appear elsewhere. For a commission, many dealers will accompany the buyer to an auction to examine any coins of interest and help formulate bids.

It is important to invest in old coins of proved value, rather than newer coins of promised numismatic value. Before buying a high-priced coin, confirm its market history. It is wise to buy coins that have demonstrated their worth in the marketplace. These are coins in which the demand exceeds the supply, and which have shown a consistent upward trend in value. Coins that are easy to buy and offered frequently are not as sound an investment. It is important to remember that a rare coin is worth exactly what it can be sold for—no more, no less.

DISCOVERING FUTURE RARITIES

"Sleeper" coins are those which for one reason or another are unappreciated, undervalued, and underpriced. Learning to spot these sleepers can be very profitable, as their price invariably goes up once in their value is recognized.

Listed below are tips to help the collector detect future rarities:

- Look for coins with high mintage figures but low relative availability. An example is an issue from which many coins may have been melted, leaving few in existence.
- Look to see what coins are not readily available in periodical advertisements and so forth.
- Take the time to specialize in a series and learn the various distinctions of the coins.
- Attend coin shows and conventions to determine which coins are commonly displayed in exhibits and which are not.
- Read everything you can about what may become tomorrow's scarce coin and why, and then form an opinion of your own.

8.

SELLING A
COIN COLLECTION

In order to sell a coin collection one must first determine its value. If it is worth only a few hundred dollars, an outright sale is the best. If it is a collection priced in excess of several thousand dollars, the story is then entirely different.

In the first place, every collector should make arrangements for the sale of his collection while he is still actively collecting. Since he has dealt—and is dealing—with many large dealers, he is in a good position to form an opinion as to whether he may trust certain dealers as potential buyers or selling agents. This information should be passed on to the collector's heirs. The sale of a collection of size must depend upon a relationship of absolute trust the collector has established with the dealer purchasing it or handling the sale. There are many honest dealers in this country, but there are a few others who will use all kinds of slick tricks to get the most for the least amount of money.

Upon the death of a collector, the first step should be the appraisal of his collection in order to determine the amount of state and federal inheritance taxes payable. Appraisals can produce both a low wholesale and a high retail valuation. Expert appraisers should give both the wholesale and retail valuations. For inheritance-tax purposes a figure between the two should be used. It is advisable not to declare too low an appraisal valuation, because then when the collection is sold there would be a much higher capital-gains tax, which would be costlier than paying a higher inheritance tax.

Your choice of an appraiser is very important. Get the best and, to your knowledge, the most honest. Pay his fee rather than accept a free appraisal. This keeps you from being obligated to any one person in the event of a sale and should get you a more accurate appraisal. There is a great temptation for appraisers to keep values low on free appraisals because they often desire to purchase the collections themselves. An appraiser should be a disinterested party, not the prospective purchaser of the collection or his agent.

Next we come to the manner of selling—whether it is outright for cash, or at auction. If selling a collection outright to a dealer, one should expect to receive between 50 and 70 percent of its retail sales value. This does not mean the guidebook or catalog value, but the actual amount for which the coins would sell. This will vary considerably from guidebook prices, depending upon what the collection contains.

Proofs and key rarities usually retail for as much as full guidebook prices, and in many instances for amounts considerably above these valuations. Extreme rarities in great demand can go at two, three, and even ten times catalog value. Circulated coins of the commoner variety, even ordinary uncirculated coins, rarely sell up to guidebook valuations; usually they sell at from 20 to 40 percent below them.

The discount of 30 to 50 percent from retail value the dealer will pay depends upon the type of material the collection contains and the amount of work involved in selling it. One must always remember that a dealer is in business to earn his living and is entitled to his profit for his efforts.

Now we come to selling at an auction. This is the manner in which all of the leading collections are sold. It has advantages and disadvantages. While cash advances on a consignment can usually be obtained, the final settlement is often slower than a cash sale because of the length of time it takes to handle the sale. One advantage is that the auctioneer is very eager to realize as much as possible for the collection. The more he can realize, the more his commission will be. He will catalog the coins to their best advantage, and hidden or unknown rarities that otherwise might not be mentioned in an outright sale will be featured in the endavor to get the most for the collection.

Surprises also occur which even conscientious dealers might not expect when purchasing outright. A coin that a dealer would normally purchase for full guidebook price, suspecting it would sell for considerably more, sold recently at auction for three times the guidebook price.

Other advantages of the auction method include a complete printed and published record of the collection in the catalog. Also, a complete printed and priced list is made of what the collection brought for every lot. And finally, if requested, the name of the collector is published in conjunction with the sale, crediting him for his efforts in compiling the collection.

The auction method does take time. It will take the cataloger about a month to prepare the catalog. It will take another month for the catalog to be printed and mailed. Another four to six weeks usually pass to allow the collectors and dealers to send in their bids. At the completion of the sale, it takes approximately one month more for payments to come in on the lots sold. Therefore, one can expect to have settlement in full thirty days after the completion of the auction sale.

The fee an auctioneer gets for his services ranges from 10 to 25 percent of the prices realized and should cover all costs, such as insurance, advertising, and printing.

Inexperienced people sometimes fear the auction method, afraid the coins will sell for a price far below their value. This is not the case. Auctioneers who run large, nationwide sales cover the market so completely—with knowledge of both dealers and collectors—that there is little opportunity for any lot to go for a ridiculous price. Sometimes an unpopular item sells at a price that appears to be quite cheap, but that is usually the true value of the coin.

The best auctions are those run by dealers who have specialized in this particular selling method for many years. In so doing, they have built up a clientele and a reputation which encourages good bidding. The best sales are a combination of mail bids and then a public sale commencing with the highest mail bid. This system, which encourages competition, brings the best prices, and the prices realized are publicly announced.

Watch out for the following when selling for cash:

Downgrading. Downgrading is listing or grading coins as inferior to what they actually are.

Selective indifference. A common practice among slick dealers is to push the choice pieces aside, concentrate on a few common ones, pay a good price for these, and get the real rare coins for a song.

Intimidation. Many a gold coin has been purchased, under threat of penalty for owning (a law long since repealed), at as low as half face value.

Omission. Many rare coins have been sold for a song simply because the experienced purchaser fails to mention that they are rare and buys a mixed collection as a "lot."

Watch out for the following when selling at auction:

High cash advances, too-low commission charges. High cash advances and too-low commission charges are inducements that are likely to work to your disadvantage. They are come-ons to get your coins.

Local club auctions. These are honest sales, but they do not draw the number of bidders necessary to bring good prices. Often a good percentage of the items are returned unsold, because a minimum bid has been offered and then no one will take up the bidding. And a majority of the coins that are sold go for the minimum, which may be very low.

Part-time auctioneers. They do not have the clientele or experience to do a good job selling your collection. It takes many years of experience to catalog correctly, build a reputation, and get lots of active bidding from both dealers and collectors.

It's not very nice to consign a collection to a dealer for outright sale of auction and have to wait and wait to get paid. If it's a cash sale, don't take it in installments. That can go on for years, the cream may then be gone, and you may have to take back what's left unsold.

Check the promptness with which your auctioneer will pay. One collector sold an $80,000 collection at an auction and had to travel 700 miles each month to get a $10,000 payment, when he should have been paid outright within thirty days of sale.

Part Two:

THE COINS LISTED

ABBREVIATIONS USED IN THE COIN VALUE LISTS

Unc.—Uncirculated
Ex. Fine—Extremely Fine
V. Fine—Very Fine
V. Good—Very Good

9.
GOLD COMMEMORATIVE COINS
(Dollar unless otherwise specified)

	Mintage in Thousands	Ex. Fine	Unc.
1903 Louisiana Purchase (Jefferson)	18	370.00	—
1903 Louisiana Purchase (McKinley)	18	370.00	—
1904 Lewis and Clark Exposition	10	495.00	—
1905 Lewis and Clark Exposition	10	495.00	—
1915S Panama-Pacific Exposition	15	180.00	—
1915S Panama-Pacific Exposition ($2.50)	7	180.00	—
1915S Panama-Pacific Exposition ($50 round)	483 Pieces	24,500.00	—
1915S Panama-Pacific Exposition ($50 octagonal)	645 Pieces	18,500.00	—
1916 McKinley Memorial	10	330.00	—
1917 McKinley Memorial	10	365.00	—
1922 Grant Memorial (with star)	5	315.00	—
1922 Grant Memorial (no star)	5	79.00	—
1926 Philadelphia Sesquicentennial ($2.50)	46	51.00	—

	Unc.	Proof
1984 Los Angeles Olympic Gold Eagle ($10)	—	—
1986W Statue of Liberty	—	155.00
1987W Constitution Bicentennial	—	110.00
1988W Olympiad—1988	130.00	130.00
1989W Gold Congressional	165.00	170.00

10.

GOLD DOLLARS—
1849–1889

LIBERTY HEAD TYPE

	Mintage in Thousands	V. Fine	Unc.
1849	689	155.00	645.00
1849C	12	425.00	1,750.00
1849D	22	375.00	3,000.00
1849O	215	195.00	1,400.00
1850	482	140.00	430.00
1850C	7	375.00	2,400.00
1850D	8	475.00	3,250.00
1850O	14	225.00	1,300.00
1851	3,318	140.00	430.00
1851C	41	425.00	1,550.00
1851D	10	425.00	3,250.00
1851O	290	200.00	1,400.00
1852	2,045	140.00	430.00
1852C	9	550.00	2,400.00
1852D	6	675.00	3,250.00
1852O	140	200.00	1,400.00
1853	4,076	140.00	430.00
1853C	12	425.00	1,750.00
1853D	7	425.00	3,250.00
1853O	290	150.00	1,425.00
1854 Small Planchet	737	140.00	430.00
1854D	3	550.00	5,500.00
1854S	15	220.00	2,600.00

INDIAN HEADDRESS TYPE

	Mintage in Thousands	V. Fine	Unc.
1954 Large Planchet	903	270.00	4,150.00
1855	758	270.00	4,150.00
1855C	10	625.00	8,750.00
1855D	2	3,000.00	17,500.00
1855O	55	575.00	8,250.00
1856S	25	510.00	8,000.00

LARGER INDIAN HEADDRESS TYPE

	Mintage in Thousands	V. Fine	Unc.	Proof
1856	1,763	135.00	395.00	—
1856D	1	3,000.00	14,500.00	—
1857	775	135.00	395.00	—
1857C	13	475.00	2,150.00	—
1857D	4	725.00	3,750.00	—
1857S	10	325.00	1,550.00	—
1858	118	135.00	395.00	19,000.00
1858D	3	725.00	4,250.00	—
1858S	10	240.00	1,400.00	—
1859	168	135.00	395.00	18,000.00
1859C	5	475.00	2,350.00	—
1859D	5	725.00	3,500.00	—
1859S	15	210.00	2,250.00	—
1860	37	135.00	395.00	18,000.00
1860D	2	2,750.00	15,000.00	—
1860S	13	325.00	1,325.00	—
1861	527	135.00	395.00	18,000.00
1861D	—	6,000.00	22,500.00	—
1862	1,361	135.00	395.00	18,000.00
1863	6	325.00	4,500.00	18,000.00
1864	6	325.00	3,200.00	18,000.00
1865	4	325.00	3,500.00	18,000.00
1866	7	325.00	1,750.00	18,000.00
1867	5	325.00	2,200.00	18,000.00
1868	11	325.00	1,600.00	18,000.00
1869	6	330.00	1,800.00	18,000.00

	Mintage in Thousands	V. Fine	Unc.	Proof
1870	6	325.00	1,800.00	18,000.00
1870S	3	800.00	3,750.00	—
1871	4	350.00	1,750.00	18,000.00
1872	4	350.00	1,900.00	18,000.00
1873	125	200.00	1,550.00	18,000.00
1874	199	135.00	395.00	19,000.00
1875	420 Pieces	2,500.00	9,750.00	20,000.00
1876	3	330.00	1,700.00	18,000.00
1877	4	350.00	1,850.00	18,000.00
1878	3	350.00	1,850.00	18,000.00
1879	3	350.00	1,750.00	18,000.00
1880	2	350.00	1,500.00	18,000.00
1881	8	325.00	1,150.00	18,000.00
1882	5	325.00	1,350.00	18,000.00
1883	11	170.00	1,350.00	18,000.00
1884	6	250.00	1,350.00	18,000.00
1885	12	170.00	1,350.00	18,000.00
1886	6	250.00	1,350.00	18,000.00
1887	9	325.00	1,350.00	18,000.00
1888	16	135.00	395.00	18,000.00
1889	31	135.00	395.00	18,000.00

11.
QUARTER EAGLES—
1796–1929

($2.50 GOLD PIECES)
LIBERTY CAP TYPE

1796

1796–1807

	Mintage in Thousands	V. Fine	Unc.
1796 No Stars	1	15,000.00	46,000.00
1796 Stars	432 Pieces	12,000.00	36,000.00
1797	427 Pieces	8,000.00	20,000.00
1798	1	4,000.00	17,000.00
1802 over 1	3	4,000.00	15,500.00
1804	3	4,000.00	15,500.00
1805	2	3,750.00	15,500.00
1806 over 4	2	2,500.00	15,500.00
1806 over 5	2	5,500.00	18,000.00
1807	7	4,000.00	15,500.00

TURBAN HEAD TYPE

1808

1821–1834

		V. Fine	Unc.
1808	3	13,000.00	50,000.00
1821	6	4,250.00	16,200.00
1824 over 21	3	4,250.00	16,200.00
1825	4	4,250.00	16,200.00
1826 over 25	1	6,000.00	30,000.00
1827	3	3,000.00	16,000.00
1829	3	3,000.00	13,500.00
1830	5	3,500.00	14,000.00
1831	5	3,500.00	14,000.00
1832	4	3,500.00	14,000.00
1833	4	3,500.00	14,000.00
1834 With Motto	4	6,000.00	30,000.00

CLASSIC HEAD TYPE

	Mintage in Thousands	Ex. Fine	Unc.
1834 No Motto	112	450.00	2,250.00
1835	131	450.00	2,250.00
1836	548	450.00	2,250.00
1837	45	450.00	2,800.00
1838	47	475.00	2,800.00
1838C	8	1,200.00	6,250.00
1839	27	325.00	2,800.00
1839C	18	650.00	5,750.00
1839D	14	1,300.00	5,275.00
1839O	18	650.00	4,500.00

CORONET TYPE

	Mintage in Thousands	Ex. Fine	Unc.
1840	19	350.00	1,400.00
1840C	13	775.00	3,000.00
1840D	4	2,500.00	5,750.00
1840O	34	350.00	1,575.00
1841 Proof (Ex. rare)	—	—	—
1841C	10	750.00	2,200.00
1841D	4	1,500.00	5,000.00
1842	3	800.00	—
1842C	7	850.00	—
1842D	5	1,250.00	—
1842O	20	500.00	—
1843	101	300.00	900.00
1843C	26	800.00	2,000.00
1843D	36	850.00	2,250.00
1843O	364	300.00	850.00
1844	7	500.00	1,800.00
1844C	12	600.00	2,250.00
1844D	17	800.00	2,500.00
1845	91	300.00	750.00

	Mintage in Thousands	Ex. Fine	Unc.	Proof
1845D	19	800.00	3,250.00	—
1845O	4	1,400.00	9,000.00	—
1846	22	350.00	1,200.00	—
1846C	5	1,000.00	3,500.00	—
1846D	19	850.00	3,250.00	—
1846O	66	250.00	1,200.00	—
1847	30	250.00	1,100.00	—
1847C	23	500.00	2,250.00	—
1847D	16	850.00	2,750.00	—
1847O	124	300.00	1,500.00	—
1848	7	700.00	2,500.00	—
1848 CAL above Eagle	1	7,500.00	29,500.00	—
1848C	17	550.00	2,250.00	—
1848D	14	850.00	2,500.00	—
1849	23	300.00	1,100.00	—
1849C	10	700.00	2,300.00	—
1849D	11	900.00	3,000.00	—
1850	253	250.00	1,200.00	—
1850C	9	750.00	2,300.00	—
1850D	12	850.00	2,500.00	—
1850O	84	250.00	1,000.00	—
1851	1,373	250.00	1,100.00	—
1851C	15	700.00	2,100.00	—
1851D	11	850.00	2,500.00	—
1851O	148	250.00	1,100.00	—
1852	1,160	250.00	700.00	—
1852C	8	800.00	2,800.00	—
1852D	4	1,200.00	3,700.00	—
1852O	140	250.00	1,000.00	—
1853	1,405	250.00	675.00	—
1853D	3	1,200.00	3,500.00	—
1854	596	250.00	1,200.00	—
1854C	7	700.00	2,500.00	—
1854D	2	4,000.00	9,500.00	—
1854O	153	250.00	1,250.00	—
1854S (Rare)	246 Pieces	—	—	—
1855	235	250.00	650.00	—
1855C	4	1,500.00	—	—
1855D	1	4,500.00	15,000.00	—
1856	384	250.00	1,100.00	—
1856C	10	750.00	2,500.00	—
1856D	1	8,500.00	20,000.00	—
1856O	21	250.00	1,250.00	—
1856S	71	250.00	1,250.00	—
1857	214	250.00	1,250.00	—
1857D	2	1,100.00	4,000.00	—
1857O	34	350.00	1,000.00	—
1857S	69	300.00	1,400.00	—
1858	47	250.00	900.00	15,000.00
1858C	9	650.00	2,000.00	—
1859	39	250.00	400.00	12,000.00
1859D	2	1,000.00	3,500.00	—
1859S	15	300.00	1,100.00	—
1860	23	250.00	1,000.00	8,000.00
1860C	7	750.00	2,500.00	—
1860S	36	300.00	1,200.00	—
1861	1,248	250.00	750.00	8,000.00

	Mintage in Thousands	Ex. Fine	Unc.	Proof
1861S	24	250.00	1,000.00	7,500.00
1862	99	250.00	1,150.00	9,000.00
1862S	8	300.00	850.00	—
1863	30 Pieces	—	—	39,750.00
1863S	11	500.00	2,000.00	—
1864	3	1,900.00	6,000.00	13,000.00
1865	2	1,750.00	5,000.00	13,000.00
1865S	23	400.00	1,200.00	—
1866	3	550.00	2,000.00	10,000.00
1866S	39	375.00	1,300.00	—
1867	3	500.00	900.00	9,000.00
1867S	28	300.00	1,000.00	—
1868	4	400.00	1,500.00	9,000.00
1868S	34	300.00	1,100.00	—
1869	4	350.00	1,200.00	9,000.00
1869S	30	325.00	600.00	—
1870	5	375.00	1,300.00	9,000.00
1870S	16	350.00	1,200.00	—
1871	5	350.00	1,200.00	9,000.00
1871S	22	250.00	900.00	—
1872	3	425.00	1,200.00	9,000.00
1872S	18	250.00	800.00	—
1873	178	250.00	750.00	9,000.00
1873S	27	250.00	650.00	—
1874	4	300.00	900.00	9,000.00
1875	420 Pieces	5,000.00	9,000.00	23,000.00
1875S	12	300.00	850.00	—
1876	4	400.00	1,250.00	9,000.00
1876S	5	350.00	1,200.00	—
1877	2	700.00	2,000.00	9,000.00
1877S	35	250.00	700.00	—
1878	286	250.00	700.00	9,000.00
1878S	178	250.00	700.00	—
1879	89	250.00	700.00	9,000.00
1879S	44	250.00	700.00	—
1880	3	350.00	950.00	9,000.00
1881	1	1,500.00	4,000.00	9,500.00
1882	4	350.00	1,000.00	8,000.00
1883	2	400.00	1,000.00	8,000.00
1884	2	350.00	1,000.00	8,000.00
1885	1	1,100.00	2,750.00	9,000.00
1886	4	250.00	1,10000.00	7,500.00
1887	6	250.00	1,100.00	7,500.00
1888	16	250.00	1,100.00	7,500.00
1889	18	250.00	1,100.00	10,500.00
1890	9	300.00	1,100.00	7,000.00
1891	11	300.00	1,100.00	7,500.00
1892	3	400.00	1,100.00	7,000.00
1893	30	250.00	1,250.00	7,000.00
1894	4	350.00	1,250.00	6,500.00
1895	6	250.00	1,250.00	7,000.00
1896	19	250.00	1,250.00	7,000.00
1897	30	250.00	1,250.00	7,000.00
1898	24	250.00	1,250.00	7,000.00
1899	27	250.00	1,250.00	7,000.00
1900	67	250.00	1,250.00	6,500.00
1901	91	250.00	1,250.00	6,500.00
1902	134	250.00	1,250.00	6,500.00

	Mintage in Thousands	Ex. Fine	Unc.	Proof
1903	201	250.00	1,000.00	6,500.00
1904	161	250.00	1,000.00	6,500.00
1905	218	250.00	1,000.00	6,500.00
1906	176	250.00	1,000.00	6,500.00
1907	336	250.00	1,000.00	6,500.00

INDIAN HEAD TYPE

	Mintage in Thousands	Ex. Fine	Unc.	Proof
1908	565	7.00	25.00	445.00
1909	442	10.00	60.00	900.00
1910	493	160.00	375.00	36,000.00
1911	704	160.00	330.00	36,000.00
1911D	56	1,000.00	3,200.00	—
1912	616	165.00	375.00	36,000.00
1913	722	160.00	350.00	36,000.00
1914	240	160.00	450.00	36,000.00
1914D	448	160.00	375.00	—
1915	606	160.00	350.00	36,00.00
1925D	578	165.00	330.00	—
1926	446	160.00	330.00	—
1927	388	160.00	330.00	—
1928	416	160.00	330.00	—
1929	532	160.00	330.00	—

12.

THREE-DOLLAR GOLD PIECES—
1854–1889

	Mintage in Thousands	V. Fine	Unc.	Proof
1854	139	505.00	2,950.00	57,500.00
1854D	1	9,500.00	49,000.00	—
1854O	24	600.00	4,100.00	—
1855	51	505.00	2,950.00	—
1855S	7	760.00	5,800.00	—
1856	26	535.00	2,950.00	—
1856S	35	760.00	4,400.00	—
1857	21	535.00	2,950.00	57,500.00
1857S	14	760.00	5,200.00	—
1858	2	800.00	4,600.00	57,500.00
1859	16	22.50	110.00	5,000.00
1860	7	15.00	130.00	2,650.00
1860S	7	760.00	5,750.00	—
1861	6	34.00	200.00	2,650.00
1862	6	12.00	75.00	2,650.00
1863	5	9.00	75.00	2,650.00
1864	3	25.00	130.00	2,650.00
1865	1	18.00	75.00	1,400.00
1866	4	68.00	150.00	1,350.00
1867	3	68.00	150.00	1,350.00
1868	5	68.00	150.00	1,350.00
1869	3	170.00	380.00	1,350.00
1870	4	165.00	275.00	1,350.00
1870S (Very rare)	2 Pieces	—	—	—
1871	1	160.00	315.00	1,350.00
1872	2	190.00	390.00	1,400.00
1873	About 80 Pieces	—	—	62,000.00
1874	42	38.00	150.00	1,100.00
1875	20 Pieces	37.00	150.00	1,100.00
1876	45 Pieces	55.00	180.00	1,100.00
1877	1	680.00	1,600.00	3,650.00

	Mintage in Thousands	V. Fine	Unc.	Proof
1878	82	58.00	200.00	950.00
1879	3	14.00	80.00	800.00
1880	1	7.50	75.00	800.00
1881	1	7.50	75.00	800.00
1882	2	7.50	75.00	800.00
1883	1	7.50	75.00	800.00
1884	1	10.00	80.00	800.00
1885	1	20.00	90.00	800.00
1886	1	18.00	80.00	800.00
1887	6	5.00	70.00	800.00
1888	5	5.50	70.00	800.00
1889	2	4.50	35.00	800.00

13.

STELLAS—
1879–1880LAR
($4 GOLD PIECES)

	Mintage in Thousands	Proof-65
1879 Flowing hair................................	415 Pieces	95,000.00
1879 Coiled hair (Very rare)......................	10 Pieces	99,500.00
1880 Flowing hair (Very rare)	15 Pieces	99,500.00
1880 Coiled hair (Very rare)......................	10 Pieces	99,500.00

14.

HALF EAGLES—
1795–1929

($5 GOLD PIECES)
CAPPED BUST TYPE

1795–1798   **1795–1807**

	Mintage in Thousands	V. Fine	Unc.
1795 Small Eagle, All Kinds........................	9	8,500.00	28,000.00
1795 Large Eagle, All Kinds	9	9,000.00	32,000.00
1796 over 95	6	8,500.00	30,000.00
1797 15 Stars, Small Eagle, All Kinds	4	7,500.00	30,000.00
1797 16 Stars, Small Eagle, All Kinds	4	7,500.00	32,000.00
1797 over 95, Large Eagle	(included above)	8,000.00	24,000.00
1798 Small Eagle (Very rare)......................	—	—	—
1798 Large Eagle, 13 star reverse, All Kinds..........	25	2,000.00	9,500.00
1798 Large Eagle, 14 star reverse, All Kinds..........	25	3,000.00	15,000.00
1799..	7	2,000.00	10,000.00
1800..	38	2,000.00	10,000.00
1802 over 1	53	2,000.00	10,000.00
1803 over 2	34	2,000.00	10,000.00
1804..	30	2,000.00	10,000.00
1805..	33	2,000.00	10,000.00
1806..	64	2,000.00	10,000.00
1807..	32	2,000.00	10,000.00

LIBERTY CAP TYPE

1807–1812 **1813–1834**

	Mintage in Thousands	V. Fine	Unc.
1807	52	1,750.00	10,000.00
1808 over 7, All Kinds	56	1,750.00	10,000.00
1808, All Kinds	56	1,750.00	10,000.00
1809 over 8	34	1,750.00	10,000.00
1810	100	1,900.00	10,000.00
1811	100	1,900.00	10,000.00
1812	58	1,900.00	9,000.00
1813	95	2,000.00	12,000.00
1814 over 3	15	2,500.00	15,000.00
1815 (Rare)	1	—	—
1818	49	2,000.00	12,500.00
1819	52	—	50,000.00
1820	264	2,000.00	12,500.00
1821	35	7,000.00	25,000.00
1822 (Very rare)	18	—	—
1823	14	3,500.00	13,500.00
1824 (Rare)	17	—	—
1825 over 21, All Kinds	29	4,000.00	20,000.00
1825 over 24 (Rare), All Kinds	29	—	—
1826	18	7,000.00	28,000.00
1827 (Rare)	25	—	—
1828 over 27, All Kinds (Rare)	28	—	—
1828, All Kinds (Rare)	28	—	—
1829 (Rare)	57	—	—
1830	126	4,000.00	15,750.00
1831	141	4,000.00	15,750.00
1832	157	7,000.00	21,000.00
1833	194	4,000.00	16,000.00
1834	50	4,000.00	16,500.00

CLASSIC HEAD TYPE

	Mintage in Thousands	Ex. Fine	Unc.
1834	658	400.00	3,000.00
1835	372	400.00	3,000.00
1836	553	400.00	3,000.00
1837	207	400.00	3,000.00
1838	287	400.00	3,000.00
1838C	17	1,300.00	8,000.00
1838D	21	2,000.00	8,000.00

CORONET TYPE

1839–1865 1865–1908

	Mintage in Thousands	Fine	Ex. Fine	Unc.
1839	118	250.00	475.00	2,600.00
1839C	17	500.00	900.00	3,500.00
1839D	19	500.00	900.00	4,600.00
1840	137	250.00	360.00	2,000.00
1840C	19	500.00	850.00	3,500.00
1840D	23	600.00	1,000.00	4,200.00
1840O	40	400.00	350.00	—
1841	16	325.00	475.00	2,250.00
1841C	21	450.00	800.00	3,750.00
1841D	29	450.00	900.00	3,500.00
1841O	50 Pieces	—	—	—
1842	28	250.00	300.00	1,700.00
1842C	28	1,000.00	1,500.00	5,000.00
1842D	160	525.00	900.00	4,000.00
1842O	16	350.00	650.00	2,500.00
1843	611	225.00	360.00	1,700.00
1843C	44	400.00	800.00	2,500.00
1843D	98	450.00	850.00	3,500.00
1843O	517	300.00	500.00	2,200.00
1844	340	250.00	300.00	1,800.00
1844C	24	450.00	750.00	3,500.00
1844D	89	450.00	800.00	3,500.00
1844O	365	300.00	400.00	2,000.00
1845	417	200.00	300.00	2,000.00
1845D	90	450.00	900.00	3,250.00
1845O	41	350.00	500.00	2,000.00
1846	396	200.00	300.00	1,600.00
1846C	13	600.00	1,000.00	4,000.00
1846D	80	500.00	1,100.00	3,000.00
1846O	58	350.00	500.00	2,300.00
1847	916	200.00	250.00	1,700.00
1847C	84	500.00	750.00	2,750.00
1847D	64	425.00	750.00	3,000.00
1847O	12	250.00	1,000.00	—
1848	261	200.00	300.00	1,800.00

	Mintage in Thousands	Fine	Ex. Fine	Unc.	Proof
1848C	64	500.00	800.00	3,000.00	—
1848D	47	500.00	900.00	3,500.00	—
1849	133	200.00	300.00	1,700.00	—
1849C	65	500.00	800.00	3,000.00	—
1849D	39	500.00	800.00	3,500.00	—
1850	64	200.00	300.00	1,600.00	—
1850C	64	500.00	800.00	3,000.00	—
1850D	44	500.00	850.00	3,200.00	—
1851	378	225.00	300.00	1,500.00	—
1851C	49	500.00	800.00	3,000.00	—
1851D	63	500.00	850.00	3,000.00	—
1851O	41	400.00	500.00	2,500.00	—
1852	574	200.00	300.00	1,250.00	—
1852C	73	500.00	850.00	3,000.00	—
1852D	92	500.00	850.00	3,000.00	—
1853	306	200.00	300.00	1,200.00	—
1853C	66	500.00	800.00	2,750.00	—
1853D	90	500.00	850.00	3,000.00	—
1854	161	200.00	275.00	1,100.00	—
1854C	39	500.00	800.00	3,000.00	—
1854D	56	500.00	1,100.00	3,500.00	—
1854O	46	350.00	500.00	2,250.00	—
1854S (Rare)	268 Pieces	—	—	—	—
1855	117	225.00	300.00	1,100.00	—
1855C	40	500.00	800.00	3,000.00	—
1855D	22	500.00	800.00	3,000.00	—
1855O	11	500.00	850.00	3,500.00	—
1855S	61	300.00	500.00	2,000.00	—
1856	198	225.00	300.00	1,100.00	—
1856C	28	500.00	800.00	3,000.00	—
1856D	20	500.00	800.00	3,000.00	—
1856O	10	525.00	900.00	—	—
1856S	105	200.00	300.00	1,100.00	—
1857	98	200.00	300.00	1,100.00	—
1857C	31	500.00	800.00	3,000.00	—
1857D	17	500.00	800.00	3,000.00	—
1857O	13	500.00	800.00	—	—
1857S	87	250.00	300.00	1,100.00	—
1858	15	250.00	400.00	1,800.00	—
1858C	39	500.00	800.00	3,000.00	—
1858D	15	500.00	800.00	3,000.00	—
1858S	19	400.00	800.00	—	—
1859	17	350.00	500.00	1,700.00	12,500.00
1859C	32	500.00	800.00	3,000.00	—
1859D	10	500.00	1,100.00	3,500.00	—
1859S	13	300.00	550.00	—	—
1860	20	300.00	550.00	1,700.00	15,000.00
1860C	15	500.00	800.00	2,750.00	—
1860D	15	500.00	900.00	4,000.00	—
1860S	21	450.00	900.00	2,000.00	—
1861	688	225.00	300.00	1,200.00	15,000.00
1861C	7	1,000.00	2,200.00	7,500.00	—
1861D	2	4,000.00	7,500.00	22,500.00	—
1861S	18	400.00	800.00	22,500.00	—
1862	4	400.00	800.00	22,500.00	15,000.00
1862S	10	400.00	1,500.00	22,500.00	—
1863	2	650.00	1,500.00	3,500.00	15,000.00
1863S	17	350.00	1,250.00	2,750.00	—

	Mintage in Thousands	V. Fine	Ex. Fine	Unc.	Proof
1864	4	450.00	700.00	4,000.00	15,000.00
1864S	4	1,000.00	2,500.00	—	—
1865	1	800.00	1,200.00	—	15,000.00
1865S	28	500.00	1,100.00	—	—
1866S No Motto	9	500.00	1,100.00	—	—
1866 Motto on Reverse	7	400.00	1,500.00	—	12,500.00
1866S	35	325.00	1,400.00	2,000.00	—
1867	7	400.00	650.00	2,000.00	12,500.00
1867S	29	350.00	600.00	2,000.00	—
1868	6	350.00	600.00	2,000.00	12,500.00
1868S	52	300.00	500.00	2,000.00	—
1869	2	700.00	950.00	2,000.00	11,000.00
1869S	31	300.00	650.00	2,000.00	—
1870	4	350.00	700.00	2,000.00	12,000.00
1870CC	7	2,500.00	4,000.00	2,000.00	—
1870S	17	300.00	600.00	2,000.00	—
1871	3	400.00	700.00	1,100.00	12,000.00
1871CC	21	700.00	1,200.00	—	—
1871S	25	250.00	500.00	3,250.00	—
1872	2	550.00	900.00	2,500.00	12,000.00
1872CC	17	700.00	1,100.00	—	—
1872S	36	300.00	450.00	—	—
1873	112	175.00	250.00	600.00	11,500.00
1873CC	7	700.00	1,200.00	3,000.00	—
1873S	31	400.00	800.00	2,000.00	—
1874	4	450.00	850.00	2,500.00	11,500.00
1874CC	21	450.00	750.00	2,500.00	—
1874S	16	300.00	550.00	—	—
1875	220 Pieces	Rare	Rare	Rare	Rare
1875CC	12	500.00	1,000.00	—	—
1875S	9	400.00	1,000.00	2,500.00	—
1876	1	600.00	1,000.00	2,500.00	950.00
1876CC	7	600.00	1,000.00	2,750.00	—
1876S	4	800.00	1,750.00	—	—
1877	1	600.00	1,000.00	3,500.00	11,000.00
1877CC	9	600.00	1,000.00	3,000.00	—
1877S	27	200.00	300.00	—	—
1878	132	200.00	200.00	375.00	12,000.00
1878CC	9	1,750.00	2,700.00	—	—
1878S	145	200.00	225.00	375.00	—
1879	302	200.00	225.00	375.00	11,000.00
1879CC	17	400.00	500.00	1,800.00	—
1879S	426	200.00	225.00	350.00	—
1880	3,166	200.00	225.00	350.00	10,000.00
1880CC	51	250.00	600.00	1,400.00	—
1880S	1,349	200.00	225.00	350.00	—
1881	5,709	200.00	225.00	350.00	9,500.00
1881CC	14	400.00	600.00	2,000.00	—
1881S	969	200.00	200.00	350.00	—
1882	2,515	200.00	250.00	350.00	9,500.00
1882CC	83	250.00	350.00	1,100.00	—
1882S	970	200.00	225.00	350.00	—
1883	233	200.00	225.00	350.00	9,500.00
1883CC	13	350.00	600.00	1,250.00	—
1883S	83	200.00	225.00	350.00	—
1884	191	200.00	225.00	350.00	9,500.00
1884CC	16	400.00	650.00	1,300.00	—
1884S	177	200.00	225.00	350.00	—

73

	Mintage in Thousands	Fine	Ex. Fine	Unc.	Proof
1885	602	200.00	225.00	450.00	9,500.00
1885S	1212	200.00	225.00	450.00	—
1886	388	200.00	225.00	450.00	9,500.00
1886S	3268	200.00	225.00	450.00	—
1887	87 Pieces	—	—	—	25,000.00
1887S	1912	200.00	225.00	350.00	—
1888	18	200.00	225.00	350.00	9,000.00
1888S	294	200.00	225.00	350.00	—
1889	8	300.00	475.00	1,300.00	9,000.00
1890	4	300.00	600.00	1,500.00	9,000.00
1890CC	54	200.00	350.00	850.00	—
1891	61	200.00	225.00	350.00	9,000.00
1891CC	208	250.00	300.00	775.00	—
1892	754	200.00	225.00	350.00	9,000.00
1892CC	83	225.00	300.00	850.00	—
1892O	10	700.00	900.00	3,000.00	—
1892S	298	200.00	225.00	350.00	—
1893	1528	200.00	225.00	350.00	9,500.00
1893CC	60	250.00	300.00	1,100.00	—
1893O	110	250.00	300.00	1,100.00	—
1893S	224	200.00	225.00	350.00	—
1894	958	200.00	225.00	350.00	9,000.00
1894O	17	250.00	400.00	1,000.00	—
1894S	56	200.00	225.00	350.00	—
1895	1346	200.00	225.00	350.00	9,000.00
1895S	112	200.00	225.00	350.00	—
1896	59	200.00	225.00	350.00	9,000.00
1896S	155	200.00	225.00	350.00	—
1897	868	200.00	225.00	350.00	9,000.00
1897S	354	200.00	225.00	350.00	—
1898	633	200.00	225.00	350.00	9,000.00
1898S	1397	200.00	225.00	350.00	—
1899	1711	200.00	225.00	300.00	9,000.00
1899S	1545	200.00	225.00	350.00	—
1900	1406	200.00	225.00	350.00	9,000.00
1900S	329	200.00	225.00	350.00	—
1901	616	200.00	225.00	350.00	9,000.00
1901S	3648	200.00	225.00	350.00	—
1902	173	200.00	225.00	350.00	9,000.00
1902S	939	200.00	225.00	350.00	—
1903	227	200.00	225.00	350.00	9,000.00
1903S	1855	200.00	225.00	350.00	—
1904	392	200.00	225.00	350.00	9,000.00
1904S	97	700.00	225.00	350.00	—
1905	302	200.00	225.00	350.00	9,000.00
1905S	881	200.00	225.00	350.00	—
1906	349	200.00	225.00	350.00	9,000.00
1906D	320	200.00	225.00	350.00	—
1906S	598	200.00	225.00	350.00	—
1907	626	200.00	225.00	350.00	9,000.00
1907D	888	200.00	225.00	350.00	—
1908	422	200.00	225.00	350.00	9,000.00

INDIAN HEAD TYPE

	Mintage in Thousands	Ex. Fine	Unc.	Proof
1908	578	7.00	25.00	445.00
1908D	148	225.00	760.00	—
1908S	82	50.00	150.00	—
1909	627	10.00	60.00	900.00
1909D	3,424	215.00	390.00	—
1909O	34	900.00	6,500.00	—
1909S	297	190.00	325.00	—
1910	604	160.00	375.00	36,000.00
1910D	194	265.00	765.00	—
1910S	770	350.00	1,900.00	—
1911	915	160.00	330.00	36,000.00
1911D	73	1,000.00	3,200.00	—
1911S	1,416	265.00	990.00	—
1912	790	165.00	375.00	36,000.00
1912S	392	265.00	1,700.00	—
1913	916	160.00	350.00	36,000.00
1913S	408	350.00	2,900.00	—
1914	247	160.00	450.00	36,000.00
1914D	247	160.00	375.00	—
1914S	263	225.00	1,000.00	—
1915	588	160.00	350.00	36,000.00
1915S	164	325.00	2,650.00	—
1916S	240	225.00	875.00	—
1929	662	160.00	330.00	—

15.
EAGLES—
1795–1933

($10 GOLD PIECES)
BUST TYPE

1795–1797   **1797–1804**

	Mintage in Thousands	V. Fine	Unc.
1795	6	8,000.00	31,000.00
1796	4	8,000.00	30,000.00
1797 Small Eagle	4	8,000.00	31,000.00
1797 Large Eagle	11	3,000.00	15,000.00
1798 over 97, 9 Stars Left, 4 Right	1	—	—
1798 over 97, 7 Stars Left, 6 Right	1	—	—
1799	37	2,500.00	14,000.00
1800	6	2,750.00	15,000.00
1801	44	2,500.00	14,000.00
1803	15	2,750.00	15,000.00
1804	4	3,500.00	18,000.00

CORONET TYPE

	Mintage in Thousands	Ex. Fine	Unc.
1838 .	7	1,600.00	8,500.00
1839 .	38	1,100.00	7,500.00

1840–1865   1866–1907

	Mintage	Ex. Fine	Unc.
1840 .	47	475.00	4,000.00
1841 .	63	475.00	4,000.00
1841O .	3	1,500.00	6,500.00
1842 .	82	475.00	4,000.00
1842O .	27	475.00	4,000.00
1843 .	75	475.00	4,000.00
1843O .	175	475.00	4,000.00
1844 .	6	950.00	5,000.00
1844O .	119	450.00	3,500.00
1845 .	26	475.00	3,500.00
1845O .	48	475.00	3,000.00
1846 .	20	475.00	3,000.00
1846O .	82	475.00	3,000.00
1847 .	862	400.00	2,500.00
1847O .	572	450.00	2,500.00
1848 .	145	325.00	2,000.00
1848O .	36	550.00	3,000.00
1849 .	654	400.00	2,000.00
1849O .	24	550.00	3,000.00
1850 .	291	400.00	2,000.00
1850O .	58	550.00	3,000.00
1851 .	176	450.00	2,200.00
1851O .	263	450.00	2,100.00
1852 .	263	425.00	2,000.00

	Mintage in Thousands	Ex. Fine	Unc.	Proof
1852O	18	600.00	3,000.00	—
1853	201	400.00	2,000.00	—
1853O	51	550.00	3,000.00	—
1854	54	500.00	2,500.00	—
1854O	53	450.00	3,000.00	—
1854S	124	450.00	2,500.00	—
1855	122	400.00	2,000.00	—
1855O	18	600.00	2,750.00	—
1855S	9	1,500.00	4,500.00	—
1856	60	400.00	2,750.00	—
1856O	15	600.00	3,250.00	—
1856S	68	500.00	2,750.00	—
1857	17	500.00	2,750.00	—
1857O	6	1,500.00	—	—
1857S	26	450.00	2,750.00	—
1858	3	6,500.00	—	—
1858O	20	450.00	3,500.00	—
1858S	12	600.00	3,500.00	—
1859	16	600.00	3,500.00	25,000.00
1859O	2	3,750.00	—	—
1859S	7	2,000.00	3,500.00	—
1860	15	600.00	3,500.00	20,000.00
1860O	11	600.00	4,000.00	—
1860S	5	1,500.00	5,500.00	—
1861	113	400.00	2,500.00	20,000.00
1861S	16	450.00	3,000.00	—
1862	11	800.00	3,000.00	20,000.00
1862S	13	450.00	3,000.00	—
1863	1	4,500.00	8,500.00	25,000.00
1863S	10	900.00	3,300.00	—
1864	4	1,500.00	5,000.00	25,000.00
1864S	3	4,000.00	—	—
1865	4	1,400.00	5,000.00	22,000.00
1865S	17	1,800.00	5,000.00	—
1866S No Motto	9	2,000.00	—	—
1866 With Motto	4	700.00	—	20,000.00
1866S	12	600.00	2,000.00	—
1867	3	700.00	—	15,000.00
1867S	9	700.00	1,850.00	—
1868	11	650.00	1,400.00	15,000.00
1868S	14	650.00	1,400.00	—
1869	2	1,750.00	3,000.00	15,000.00
1869S	6	750.00	1,750.00	—
1870	4	800.00	2,200.00	15,000.00
1870CC	6	3,500.00	—	—
1870S	8	850.00	—	—
1871	2	1,500.00	—	15,000.00
1871CC	7	1,500.00	—	—
1871S	17	600.00	1,400.00	—
1872	2	1,900.00	—	12,000.00
1872CC	6	1,100.00	—	—
1872S	17	600.00	—	—
1873	1	3,000.00	—	22,000.00
1873CC	5	2,250.00	5,500.00	—
1873S	12	600.00	1,400.00	—
1874	53	400.00	750.00	18,500.00
1874CC	17	650.00	2,000.00	—

	Mintage in Thousands	Ex. Fine	Unc.	Proof
1874S	10	550.00	1,500.00	—
1875 (Very rare)	120 Pieces	—	—	—
1875CC	8	1,000.00	3,000.00	—
1876	1	3,000.00	8,000.00	17,500.00
1876CC	5	1,500.00	3,750.00	—
1876S	5	800.00	2,500.00	—
1877	1	3,500.00	9,000.00	20,000.00
1877CC	3	2,000.00	4,000.00	—
1877S	17	500.00	1,000.00	—
1878	74	350.00	600.00	15,750.00
1878CC	3	2,000.00		—
1878S	26	500.00	650.00	—
1879	385	325.00	375.00	15,750.00
1879CC	2	5,000.00	—	—
1879O	2	2,500.00	8,000.00	—
1879S	224	325.00	425.00	—
1880	1,645	325.00	425.00	13,500.00
1880CC	11	550.00	1,350.00	—
1880O	9	500.00	1,250.00	—
1880S	506	350.00	425.00	—
1881	3,877	325.00	425.00	13,500.00
1881CC	24	500.00	1,200.00	—
1881O	8	500.00	1,250.00	—
1881S	970	350.00	400.00	—
1882	2,324	350.00	425.00	13,500.00
1882CC	17	550.00	1,650.00	—
1882O	11	500.00	950.00	—
1882S	132	350.00	450.00	—
1883	209	350.00	425.00	13,500.00
1883CC	12	600.00	1,500.00	—
1883O	1	3,750.00	12,000.00	—
1883S	38	300.00	450.00	—
1884	77	325.00	450.00	21,000.00
1884CC	10	650.00	1,500.00	—
1884S	124	350.00	500.00	—
1885	254	350.00	500.00	12,000.00
1885S	228	350.00	500.00	—
1886	236	350.00	500.00	12,000.00
1886S	826	350.00	500.00	—
1887	54	350.00	500.00	12,000.00
1887S	817	350.00	500.00	—
1888	133	350.00	500.00	12,000.00
1888O	21	350.00	500.00	—
1888S	649	350.00	500.00	—
1889	4	650.00	1,500.00	14,500.00
1889S	425	350.00	450.00	—
1890	58	350.00	450.00	11,750.00
1890CC	18	400.00	950.00	—
1891	92	350.00	450.00	11,750.00
1891CC	104	350.00	900.00	—
1892	798	350.00	450.00	11,750.00
1892CC	40	450.00	1,000.00	—
1892O	29	350.00	650.00	—
1892S	116	325.00	550.00	—
1893	1,841	325.00	550.00	11,750.00
1893CC	14	600.00	1,450.00	—
1893O	17	450.00	900.00	—

	Mintage in Thousands	Ex. Fine	Unc.	Proof
1893S	141	325.00	575.00	—
1894	2,471	300.00	500.00	11,750.00
1894O	108	300.00	450.00	—
1894S	25	300.00	550.00	—
1895	568	325.00	450.00	11,750.00
1895O	98	325.00	450.00	—
1895S	49	350.00	500.00	—
1896	76	350.00	450.00	11,750.00
1896S	124	350.00	500.00	—
1897	1,000	350.00	450.00	11,750.00
1897O	43	350.00	500.00	—
1897S	235	350.00	500.00	—
1898	812	325.00	525.00	11,250.00
1898S	474	325.00	525.00	—
1899	1,262	325.00	525.00	11,000.00
1899O	37	325.00	525.00	—
1899S	841	325.00	525.00	—
1900	294	325.00	525.00	11,500.00
1900S	81	325.00	525.00	—
1901	1,719	325.00	525.00	10,000.00
1901O	72	325.00	525.00	—
1901S	2,813	325.00	525.00	—
1902	83	325.00	525.00	10,500.00
1902S	470	325.00	525.00	—
1903	126	325.00	525.00	11,000.00
1903O	113	325.00	525.00	—
1903S	538	325.00	525.00	—
1904	162	325.00	525.00	12,000.00
1904O	109	325.00	525.00	—
1905	201	325.00	525.00	10,500.00
1905S	369	325.00	525.00	—
1906	165	325.00	525.00	11,500.00
1906D	981	325.00	525.00	—
1906O	87	325.00	525.00	—
1906S	457	325.00	525.00	—
1907, All Kinds	1,204	325.00	525.00	10,500.00
1907D	1,030	325.00	525.00	—
1907S	211	325.00	525.00	—

INDIAN HEAD TYPE

No Motto   Motto

	Mintage in Thousands	Ex. Fine	Unc.	Proof
1907 Wire Edge, Periods before and after Legends	500 Pieces	3,000	10,000.00	60,000.00
1907 Rolled Edge, Periods (Rare)	42 Pieces	—	28,000.00	99,500.00
1907 No Periods	239	575.00	625.00	—
1908 No Motto	34	585.00	950.00	—
1908D No Motto	210	575.00	750.00	—
1908 With Motto	341	7.00	25.00	445.00
1908D	837	225.00	760.00	—
1908S	60	50.00	150.00	—
1909	185	10.00	60.00	900.00
1909D	122	215.00	390.00	—
1909S	292	190.00	325.00	—
1910	319	160.00	375.00	36,000.00
1910D	2,357	265.00	765.00	—
1910S	811	350.00	1,900.00	—
1911	506	160.00	330.00	36,000.00
1911D	30	1,000.00	3,200.00	—
1911S	51	265.00	990.00	—
1912	405	165.00	375.00	36,000.00
1912S	300	265.00	1,700.00	—
1913	442	160.00	350.00	36,000.00
1913S	66	350.00	2,900.00	—
1914	151	160.00	450.00	36,000.00
1914D	344	160.00	375.00	—
1914S	208	225.00	1,000.00	—
1915	351	160.00	350.00	36,000.00
1915S	59	325.00	2,650.00	—
1916S	139	225.00	875.00	—
1920S (Rare)	127	8,000.00	15,000.00	—
1926	1,014	160.00	330.00	—
1930S	96	5,000.00	14,000.00	—
1932	4,463	425.00	480.00	—
1933 (Rare)	313	—	48,000.00	—

16.
DOUBLE EAGLES—
1850–1932

($20 GOLD PIECES)
CORONET TYPE

1849–1865   **1866–1907**

	Mintage in Thousands	Ex. Fine	Unc.
1849 Unique—U. S. Mint Collection			
1850	1,170	700.00	2,750.00
1850O	141	900.00	4,000.00
1851	2,087	700.00	1,800.00
1851O	315	900.00	4,000.00
1852	2,053	700.00	2,000.00
1852O	190	900.00	3,750.00
1853	1,261	700.00	1,900.00
1853O	71	850.00	4,500.00
1854	758	700.00	2,000.00
1854O (Rare).....................................	3	—	—
1854S	141	750.00	3,500.00
1855	365	700.00	1,750.00
1855O	8	4,000.00	—
1855S	880	650.00	2,000.00
1856	330	600.00	2,000.00
1856O (Rare).....................................	2	—	—
1856S	1,190	650.00	2,000.00
1857	439	650.00	2,000.00
1857O	30	950.00	4,750.00
1857S	971	650.00	2,000.00
1858	212	650.00	2,000.00
1858O	35	950.00	6,000.00
1858S	847	700.00	1,500.00
1859	44	700.00	3,500.00
1859O	9	3,200.00	8,500.00
1859S	636	700.00	1,750.00
1860	578	600.00	1,750.00

	Mintage in Thousands	Ex. Fine	Unc.
1860O	7	3,500.00	9,000.00
1860S	545	700.00	2,000.00
1861	2,976	700.00	1,750.00
1861O	18	2,500.00	7,750.00
1861S	768	700.00	1,750.00
1862	92	700.00	4,000.00
1862S	854	700.00	2,000.00
1863	143	700.00	4,500.00
1863S	967	700.00	2,000.00
1864	204	700.00	2,750.00
1864S	794	700.00	2,000.00
1865	351	700.00	2,000.00
1865S	1,043	700.00	2,000.00
1866S No Motto	—	950.00	4,500.00
1866 With Motto	699	650.00	2,000.00
1866S	842	650.00	2,000.00
1867	251	650.00	2,000.00
1867S	921	650.00	2,000.00
1868	99	650.00	2,200.00
1868S	838	650.00	2,000.00
1869	175	650.00	2,000.00
1869S	687	650.00	2,000.00
1870	155	650.00	1,850.00
1870CC (Very Rare)	4	—	—
1870S	982	600.00	1,500.00
1871	80	650.00	2,000.00
1871CC	17	2,500.00	—
1871S	928	650.00	1,750.00
1872	252	650.00	1,500.00
1872CC	30	950.00	3,500.00
1872S	780	650.00	850.00
1873	1,710	650.00	900.00
1873CC	22	900.00	3,000.00
1873S	1,041	650.00	900.00
1874	367	650.00	900.00
1874CC	115	850.00	2,000.00
1874S	1,241	650.00	900.00
1875	296	650.00	900.00
1875CC	111	850.00	2,000.00
1875S	1,230	650.00	900.00
1876	584	650.00	900.00
1876CC	138	800.00	1,900.00
1876S	1,597	650.00	900.00
1877	398	600.00	750.00
1877CC	43	900.00	2,000.00
1877S	1,735	600.00	750.00
1878	544	650.00	750.00
1878CC	13	1,000.00	3,000.00
1878S	1,739	600.00	700.00
1879	208	600.00	700.00
1879CC	11	1,750.00	4,500.00
1879O	2	3,800.00	12,500.00
1879S	1,224	600.00	700.00
1880	51	600.00	750.00
1880S	836	600.00	750.00
1881	2	4,500.00	12,500.00
1881S	727	600.00	750.00

	Mintage in Thousands	Ex. Fine	Unc.
1882	1	10,000.00	33,000.00
1882CC	39	850.00	1,750.00
1882S	1,125	600.00	750.00
1883 (Rare)	92 Pieces	—	—
1883CC	60	850.00	1,750.00
1883S	1,189	600.00	700.00
1884 (Rare)	71 Pieces	—	—
1884CC	81	850.00	1,600.00
1884S	916	600.00	750.00
1885	1	8,500.00	25,000.00
1885CC	9	1,500.00	3,750.00
1885S	684	600.00	750.00
1886	1	9,000.00	25,000.00
1887 (Rare)	121 Pieces	—	—
1887S	283	600.00	750.00
1888	226	600.00	750.00
1888S	860	600.00	750.00
1889	44	600.00	800.00
1889CC	31	750.00	1,850.00
1889S	775	600.00	750.00
1890	76	600.00	750.00
1890CC	91	750.00	1,750.00
1890S	803	600.00	750.00
1891	1	3,000.00	8,500.00
1891CC	5	2,000.00	5,750.00
1891S	1,288	650.00	700.00
1892	5	2,000.00	5,000.00
1892CC	27	925.00	2,250.00
1892S	930	600.00	700.00
1893	344	600.00	750.00
1893CC	18	900.00	2,750.00
1893S	996	600.00	750.00
1894	1,369	600.00	750.00
1894S	1,049	600.00	750.00
1895	1,115	600.00	750.00
1895S	1,144	650.00	700.00
1896	793	650.00	700.00
1896S	1,404	650.00	700.00
1897	1,383	650.00	700.00
1897S	1,470	650.00	700.00
1898	170	650.00	700.00
1898S	2,575	650.00	700.00
1899	1,669	650.00	700.00
1899S	2,010	650.00	700.00
1900	1,875	650.00	700.00
1900S	2,460	650.00	700.00
1901	112	650.00	700.00
1901S	1,596	650.00	700.00
1902	31	650.00	850.00
1902S	1,754	650.00	700.00
1903	287	600.00	750.00
1903S	954	650.00	750.00
1904	6,257	600.00	700.00
1904S	5,134	600.00	700.00
1905	59	600.00	700.00
1905S	1,813	600.00	700.00
1906	70	600.00	850.00
1906D	620	550.00	700.00

	Mintage in Thousands	Ex. Fine	Unc.
1906	70	600.00	850.00
1906D	620	550.00	700.00
1906S	2,066	550.00	700.00
1907	1,452	550.00	700.00
1907D	842	550.00	700.00
1907S	2,166	550.00	700.00

SAINT-GAUDENS TYPE

1907 High Relief Roman Numerals (MCMVII) Wire Rim, All Kinds	11	4,850.00	8,000.00
1907 High Relief Flat Rim, All Kinds	11	3,600.00	6,600.00

1907–1908   1908–1932 Motto

1907 No Motto	362	445.00	540.00
1908	4,272	445.00	500.00
1908D	664	445.00	540.00
1908 With Motto	156	445.00	600.00
1908D	350	445.00	525.00
1908S	22	1,000.00	5,400.00
1909 over 8, All Kinds	161	525.00	1,150.00
1909, All Kinds	—	460.00	660.00
1909D	53	750.00	2,050.00
1909S	2,775	460.00	540.00
1910	482	460.00	525.00
1910D	429	460.00	525.00
1910S	2,128	460.00	550.00
1911	197	460.00	580.00

	Mintage in Thousands	Ex. Fine	Unc.
1911D	847	460.00	510.00
1911S	776	470.00	535.00
1912	150	460.00	650.00
1913	169	460.00	540.00
1913D	394	460.00	510.00
1913S	34	460.00	960.00
1914	95	460.00	690.00
1914D	453	445.00	535.00
1914S	1,498	460.00	510.00
1915	152	460.00	600.00
1915S	568	460.00	510.00
1916S	796	460.00	525.00
1920	228	460.00	570.00
1920S	558	8,500.00	13,500.00
1921	530	12,000.00	22,000.00
1922	1,376	460.00	500.00
1922S	2,658	650.00	1,025.00
1923	566	460.00	500.00
1923D	1,702	525.00	590.00
1924	4,324	460.00	500.00
1924D	3,050	900.00	1,900.00
1924S	2,928	900.00	1,550.00
1925	2,832	445.00	500.00
1925D	2,939	1,100.00	2,500.00
1925S	3,777	1,000.00	2,000.00
1926	817	445.00	500.00
1926D	481	1,200.00	2,800.00
1926S	2,042	1,100.00	1,800.00
1927	2,947	445.00	490.00
1927D (Rare)	180	—	—
1927S	3,107	3,500.00	10,000.00
1928	8,816	445.00	490.00
1929	1,780	3,200.00	9,200.00
1930S	74	8,500.00	20,000.00
1931	2,938	7,500.00	14,000.00
1931D	107	6,900.00	13,500.00
1932	1,102	8,000.00	16,000.00

(Note: Nearly all dates through 1915 of Double Eagles exist in Proof; all are very rare and perfect pieces are valued upwards of $35,000.00 each.)

17.
PRIVATE AND TERRITORIAL GOLD COINS

GEORGIA

	V. Good	Ex. Fine
1830 $2.50 TEMPLETON REID (Very rare)	—	30,000.00
1830 $5.00 TEMPLETON REID (Very rare)	—	100,000.00
1830 TEN DOLLARS (Very rare)	48,000.00	—
NO DATE. TEN DOLLARS (Very rare)	30,000.00	—

NORTH CAROLINA

	Fine	Unc.
$1.00 CHRISTOPHER BECHTLER	1,000.00	2,750.00
$2.50	3,500.00	9,000.00
$5.00	3,500.00	13,000.00

CALIFORNIA
NORRIS, GRIEF AND NORRIS

1849 $5.00	2,500.00	18,000.00

MOFFAT & CO.

	V. Fine	Ex. Fine
1849 $10.00	1,000.00	4,500.00
1849 $5.00	1,200.00	2,000.00
1850 $5.00	1,100.00	2,000.00
1852 $10.00	2,000.00	7,000.00

AUGUSTUS HUMBERT
U.S. ASSAYER

	V. Fine	Ex. Fine
1851 FIFTY DOLLARS 880 THOUS. "Target" Reverse.....................................	7,000.00	13,000.00
1851 FIFTY DOLLARS 887 THOUS. "Target" Reverse.....................................	7,500.00	13,000.00
1852 FIFTY DOLLARS 887 THOUS. No "Target"	6,000.00	13,000.00
1852 FIFTY DOLLARS 900 THOUS.	5,000.00	11,000.00
1851 50 D Several Varieties: AUGUSTUS HUMBERT UNITED STATES ASSAYER OF GOLD CALIFORNIA 1851..........................	7,000.00	25,000.00
1852 TWENTY DOLLARS 1852 over 1	3,500.00	7,000.00
1853 TWENTY DOLLARS 884 THOUS.	9,000.00	12,500.00
1853 TWENTY DOLLARS 900 THOUS.	1,500.00	4,000.00

1852 TEN DOLLARS 1852 over 1	1,500.00	4,000.00
1852 TEN DOLLARS 884 THOUS.	900.00	2,500.00
1853 TEN DOLLARS 884 THOUS. (Rare)	4,000.00	11,500.00
1853 TEN DOLLARS 900 THOUS.	2,000.00	6,000.00

BALDWIN & COMPANY

	V. Fine	Unc.
1850 TEN DOLLARS.	19,000.00	—
1851 TWENTY DOLLARS (Rare).	—	—
1851 TEN DOLLARS.	9,000.00	—
1850 FIVE DOLLARS	5,000.00	16,000.00

SCHULTZ & COMPANY

1851 FIVE DOLLARS	20,000.00	37,500.00

DUNBAR & COMPANY

1851 FIVE DOLLARS (Rare)	60,000.00	—

WASS, MOLITOR & COMPANY

	Fine	Ex. Fine
1855 FIFTY DOLLARS..........................	11,000.00	25,000.00
1855 TWENTY DOLLARS, Small Head	7,000.00	16,000.00
1855 TWENTY DOLLARS, Large Head (Rare).......	—	40,000.00
1852 TEN DOLLARS, Small Head	3,500.00	8,000.00
1852 TEN DOLLARS, Large Head.................	1,500.00	5,000.00
1855 TEN DOLLARS............................	7,000.00	15,000.00
1852 FIVE DOLLARS, Small Head	2,000.00	7,000.00
1852 FIVE DOLLARS, Large Head	2,000.00	7,000.00

KELLOGG & COMPANY

	Fine	Ex. Fine
1855 FIFTY DOLLARS (Rare).....................	—	—
1854 TWENTY DOLLARS........................	1,750.00	3,500.00
1855 TWENTY DOLLARS........................	1,400.00	3,500.00

Between 1852 and 1882, round and octagonal one-dollar, fifty-cent, and twenty-five-cent gold pieces were also issued in California. After an act of 1864 made private coinage illegal, their makers were anonymous; their initials, however, can be found on some coins.

There are many copies of these small coins, some made to be worn as charms. Genuine pieces all show their denomination—"1/2 Dol.," or "1/2 Dollar," or "half dollar," etc.

These coins are valued as follows:

	Fine	Unc.
.25 Round Indian or Liberty Heads	40.00	250.00
.25 Octagonal Indian or Liberty Heads	40.00	250.00
.50 Round Indian or Liberty Heads	50.00	350.00
.50 Octagonal Indian or Liberty Heads	50.00	650.00
1.00 Round Indian Heads	550.00	2,500.00
1.00 Octagonal Indian or Liberty Heads	150.00	1,000.00
1.00 Round Liberty Heads	600.00	3,000.00
(Washington Heads bring about 50% more.)		

OREGON

OREGON EXCHANGE COMPANY

		Ex. Fine
1849 TEN DOLLARS (Rare)	25,000.00	44,000.00
1849 FIVE DOLLARS	7,500.00	16,000.00

UTAH

MORMON GOLD

	V. Fine
1849 TWENTY DOLLARS (Rare)	40,000.00
1849 TEN DOLLARS (Rare)	75,000.00

1849 FIVE DOLLARS............................ 2,500.00 5,000.00

1849 TWO AND ONE-HALF DOLLARS 3,000.00 6,500.00
1850 FIVE DOLLARS............................ 2,500.00 6,000.00

1860 FIVE DOLLARS............................ 5,000.00 12,000.00

COLORADO

CLARK, GRUBER & COMPANY

1860 TWENTY DOLLARS (Rare).................. 12,500.00 30,000.00
1860 TEN DOLLARS............................. 3,000.00   7,500.00
1861 TWENTY DOLLARS........................ 5,000.00 14,000.00

1861 TEN DOLLARS.............................	1,500.00	3,500.00
1861 FIVE DOLLARS...........................	1,500.00	3,000.00
1861 TWO AND ONE-HALF DOLLARS............	850.00	2,000.00

CLARK & CO.

1860 FIVE DOLLARS...........................	1,000.00	3,500.00
1860 TWO AND ONE-HALF DOLLARS............	850.00	2,500.00

JOHN PARSONS & COMPANY

(1861) Undated 21/2D (Rare).......................	—	35,000.00
(1861) Undated FIVE D (Rare)....................	—	50,000.00

J.J. CONWAY & COMPANY

(1861) 2-1/2 DOLL'S (Rare).......................	—	35,000.00
(1861) FIVE DOLLARS (Rare)	—	60,000.00
1861 TEN DOLLARS (Very rare)	—	—

93